GARDENER'S MAGIC AND FOLKLORE

GARDENER'S MAGIC
AND FOLKLORE

Margaret Baker

UNIVERSE BOOKS
New York

Published in the United States of America in 1978
by Universe Books
381 Park Avenue South, New York, N.Y. 10016

© Margaret Baker 1978

Library of Congress Catalog Card Number: 77-73799
ISBN 0-87663-299-1

Printed in Great Britain

CONTENTS

		page
List of Illustrations		7
Introduction		9

1 Moon, Sun and Stars — 12

The Moon's Phases · The Role of the Almanacs · '... Consult the Moon' · Above- and Below-Ground Crops · The Moon and Flowers · Planting, Grafting and Pruning Fruit-Trees · Harvesting the Crop · Weeds and Lawns: Fences and Fertilizers · Gardening by Moonlight: The Weather · The Sun's Path · Boundaries of Time · 'The Sun Leaves His Seat' · North to South: East to West · Signs of the Zodiac · Planting by the Signs · T. E. Black's System · Pros and Cons

2 Growing Magic — 43

In the Orchard · 'Meere Idle Tales and Fancies' · First Fruits · 'Put a Dead Cat Under Them' · Planting Trees · Letters to Mice · Wassailing the Orchard · 'Them's Family Matters...'. Burning the Witch · Sex and Plants · Seeds and Cuttings

3 Seasons and Saints' Days: The Rolling Year — 70

The Gate of the Year · Christmastide · St Bride, Candlemas and St Valentine · Leap Year Beans · Saints David, Chad and Patrick · Spring Weather · Blind Days and Planting Signs · The Date of Easter · Good Friday in the Garden · The Puzzle of Parsley · Potatoes and Good Friday · The Green of May · Whitsun and Gooseberry Shows · About Midsummer Day · Blessing the Apples · Fall Fairs and Flower Shows · Hallowe'en and Pumpkins · Winter Weather Signs

4 Witchcraft and the Supernatural   97
Eye, Voice and Hand · Weeds and Stones: More Curses ·
Orchard Denizens · Garden Ghosts · Trees and Plants of
Presence · Iron and Salt: Stones and Bones · The Sign of the
Cross · The Devil's Offering

5 Plants, Personalities and Predictions   127
Green Fingers and Thumbs · Plant to Plant: Plant to Owner
· Life and Death · Telling the Plants · 'Flowers out of
Season . . .' · '*Moi, Je Parle aux Pommiers* . . .' · Musical
Plants · Touching and Praying · Help from the Devas

6 Traditional Receipts   142
Soot and Tea: Boots and Beer · Eggshells and Ashes: Soap
and Tobacco · Therapeutic Plants · Moles, Mice and Birds ·
Plants for Bees and Butterflies

7 Companion Planting   157
Herbs · The Allium Family · Companion Flowers · Amiable
Vegetables

Appendix: The Calendar Change of 1752   165
References   167
Bibliography   175
Acknowledgements   177
Index   179

LIST OF ILLUSTRATIONS

Wassailing in a Devon orchard, 1851	49
A gardener at work, about 1550	50
Gardeners at Waddesdon, Buckinghamshire, 1908	50
Lily-of-the-valley	67
'Griggling'	68
Plants enjoying Bach's *Minuet in G*, Montreal, 1975	101
Pruning	101
Egton Bridge Old Gooseberry Show, Yorkshire	102
F. W. Greenslade with his 'Charm' chrysanthemum	102
Peas	119
Plums	119
Broad Beans	119
Rowan	119
Quince and mulberry	120
Sage	120
Box	120

The author and the publishers thank the following copyright-holders for permission to reproduce their photographs:
Albert Cherry, 50 (bottom); Michael Dugas: *Montreal Gazette*, 101 (top); *Illustrated London News*, 49; *The Kent and Sussex Courier*, 102 (bottom); John Tindale, 102 (top).

INTRODUCTION

Even in the late twentieth century, the age of scientific gardening, an abundance of garden beliefs remains to us. In the years 1973 to 1976, through the courtesy of newspaper and magazine editors in Britain, the Republic of Ireland and the United States, I was able to appeal for instances of gardening traditions and received many enjoyable letters from those who clearly cherish their superstitions and are eager to record them. 'Old Customs and old wives fables . . . ought not to be buried in Oblivion: there may be some truth and usefulnesse to be picked out of them,' John Aubrey wrote in the seventeenth century. Many modern gardeners would agree.

Garden folklore survives with the peculiar power of beliefs woven from memories and union with the past: a living garden is, perhaps, the most intimate gift offered by one generation to the next. Horticulture, as practised by the primitive peoples of tropical Africa, must have preceded agriculture as such: man's earliest crop tools were the digging stick and hoe, rather than the plough. Garden beliefs, so richly diverse, reflect this antiquity. Paganism modified by Christianity is readily perceived: moon and zodiac favour plant growth; propitiatory and protective rites are acknowledged. The cult of the Earth Mother or White Goddess, unobtrusive yet resilient, must be chalked up to immemorial magic. Wise gardeners are aware, as they always have been, of the dangers of slighting the Goddess; of the tributes due to her; of favours to be received. Her cult is far from dead: its twentieth-century aspect is the biodynamic gardening movement, which underlines the wisdom of co-operation with Nature, rather than her exploitation.

As it has for the 6,000 years which have elapsed since man's first

9

attempts at horticulture, the seasonal calendar offers reliable reminders
to those gardeners not fettered by the printed word. When, in earlier
years, blights—witches work?—struck as if from a clear sky, the
gardener stood vigilant with his counterblast of spells and protective
plantings. Traces of such prophylactic magic survive. Universality of
belief is a striking feature of garden lore: with subtle variations the
same superstitions and precautions appear in one culture after another,
even in countries thousands of miles apart. The folklore of growing
things is not contained by frontiers.

Today there is increasing interest in responses of plant to plant and
plant to gardener which, beginning to be accepted by science, suggest
that old beliefs concerning green thumbs and life-indexes may go far
beyond the pure superstition that they seem at first glance. Far from
being *artes perditae*, ancient remedies for pests and diseases devised by
gardeners using homely handy ingredients centuries before the arrival
of gardening by chemicals may be as effective—and are almost invariably safer—than the answers of science. The biodynamic movement has given fresh life to traditional garden receipts and companion
plantings, which are emerging again as serious aids to gardeners.

Although not of course directly interested in folklore as such,
organizations which have reassessed certain old garden practices include, in the United States, the Bio-Dynamic Farming and Gardening
Association, Inc, and, in Britain, the Henry Doubleday Research Association and the Bio-Dynamic Agricultural Association, whose work
flows from the concepts of Dr Rudolf Steiner, founder of anthro-
posophy. In his youth Dr Steiner had observed the traditional practices
of the peasant farmers of Europe and incorporated his conclusions in an
agricultural course given at Koberwitz, Germany, in 1924. The
BDAA is concerned with the interplay of invisible forces in a visible
world, with links between plants and formative influences in soil and
atmosphere, and with extraterrestrial agents such as the sun, moon
and stars.

What is to be made of this mass of garden beliefs? So apparently
contradictory, so fine-drawn the distinctions, so personal the arguments that perhaps our conclusion might be that no conclusions *are* to
be drawn. But superstitions of pedigree have been well tested by time:
'When they come to the triall, they all vanish away like smoak,' wrote

John Parkinson in a happy Elizabethan phrase. Or they survive triumphantly. In garden folklore today the message is plain. Old-time gardeners depending upon ancient secrets undoubtedly scored remarkable successes. We must ask 'Could *they* have done as well, had they ignored superstition? Can *we* do better if we heed it?' Greater knowledge will be needed before these lacunae can be filled: still, the answer to the last question might well turn out to be an emphatic 'yes'.

In this book the writer has been collector, not apologist. A vast, almost undocumented subject imposed its own selective approach: an Anglo-American bias is obvious but even so, many omissions are unavoidable, and there is perhaps less exploration of motive than the interest of the beliefs merits. A tradition concerned with making plants *grow* was generally preferred to one of plant mythology or reputation. For reasons of space only a selection of the hundreds of fascinating beliefs which correspondents described so vividly in their letters could find a place in the book, but every letter threw valuable light on one or more of the varied aspects of garden folklore, and all letters have been preserved carefully for the future.

Much of course remains to be collected. Perhaps this survey will encourage others to look out for the gardening beliefs of their own neighbourhoods.

I

MOON, SUN AND STARS

From earliest times the moon, riding serenely along her appointed road from invisible new moon to horned, gibbous and glowing full, has been the most manifest and reliable emblem of growth: man has naturally aligned his hopes for his crops with her phases. Even in the cool light of science she has, as Luna, never lost her allure for gardeners and many still pay lip service, at least, to moon planting. The loud complaints heard from the time of the Russians' first contact with the moon in 1959 until the recent American moon landings, suggest that ancient reverence for her person is not dead ('I often saw my mother bow and curtsey to the new moon,' writes a Norfolk correspondent[1]) and the superstitious are in general agreement that she 'should be left be', a handsome unprobed mystery and an aid to husbandmen. In parts of the rural United States, to neglect to plant by the signs of the zodiac is regarded as crassest folly.

The sun too has his established place in garden tradition. In their pre-planting rituals Roman gardeners prudently sacrificed to both Sol and Luna.

These cosmic assistants continue to receive their proper regard. When, for its centenary in 1976, the famous American seed house of W. Atlee Burpee Co, of Warminster, Pennsylvania, marketed an electric 'planting clock', it was made to show at a glance the time of day, day of the week, month of the year, phase of the moon, days of first and last frost and proper days for planting—all essential data for gardeners observing the traditional rules described in this book.

THE MOON'S PHASES

The 'new moon' marks the start of the lunar cycle and is reached at slightly varying intervals round a mean of 29½ days, a lunar month, during which time the moon travels once round the earth. The revolution brings her once again into the same position relative to the sun and the earth. The moon shines by reflecting the sun's light: at new moon her dark side faces the earth—she lies roughly between the earth and the sun—but as she waxes more and more of the sunlit side comes into view, until at full—when she is at the far side of the earth from the sun—the whole of her sunlit face is turned towards the earth.

In gardeners' parlance the period from new to full moon (the waxing, making or increase) is the 'light of the moon'; the period from full to new (the waning, wasting or decrease) the 'dark of the moon'. The year's moons are seasonal benchmarks. Traditionally the May moon is the 'plant moon' when trees and plants burst into leaf; the April moon is the 'germination moon', time for seed-sowing; the frosty January moon benefits ploughed soil. In the old days it was said that timber or fruit tree props cut at the solstitial December or Christmas moon when the sap was down could be relied upon to endure for ever.[2] At the nearest full moon to the autumnal equinox, most noticeably in high latitudes, for several evenings in succession the golden and glowing 'harvest moon' rises at much the same time, just as the sun sets. Daylight and full moon meet, giving extra light once acclaimed as a divine boon to aid crop gathering.

THE ROLE OF THE ALMANACS

For the first day or two of her life the moon is invisible and lest valuable time be lost the gardener wishing to take full advantage of her growth for seed-sowing and other operations refers to the traditional gardening instructions of the almanacs, which retain many dedicated followers. Earlier generations cherished them more fondly yet. C. L. Anstine of Marietta, Georgia, told the writer in 1974 that his great-grandfather, a farmer descended from Huguenots who came to Pennsylvania, passed on his knowledge of farming and gardening to his son, Mr Anstine's grandfather; and added:

Der Hagerstauner Kalender or *Baer's Agricultural Almanac* ... was a daily
guide to just about anything that one would wish to do around the farm ...
the old farmers not only planted by the moon but also butchered, cut
timber, set fences—and even cut their hair by it! If my memories of my
grandfather's abilities are accurate, there must be something to it. Without
the benefit of modern sprays or potions he was able to obtain yields which
would rival any possible today. History can be a great teacher if only we
will just listen.[3]

In America the Pennsylvanian Germans were, and still are, said to
'live by almanac and bible', and while such astrological dogma as the
almanacs propound has never lacked opponents, in rural districts it is
still comparatively easy to find a believer for every scoffer. It was much
the same in England. 'Sixty years ago when I was a boy in Kent,'
writes R. Winder of Caister St Edmund, 'the villagers sowed their
vegetables by the moon ... *Old Moore's Almanac* was to be found in
most of the cottages.'[4]

Old names and reputations survive, particularly in the United States.
The Old Farmer's Almanac, first published in 1792 for 1793, has never
openly commended astrology to its readers but nevertheless aspects of
the planets appear throughout its pages. *The Daboll Almanac*, said to
have been published without break since 1772, *Leavitt's Almanac* in
New Hampshire, *Grier's Almanac* in Georgia, first published in 1807,
and *Francis and Lusky's wall calendar* published in Nashville, Tennessee,
with sun, moon and zodiacal data, are well-known names. Some
almanacs have exhibited local accents—and special followings: of this
kind are *Belcher's Nova Scotia Farmer's Almanac*, established in 1824, and
Robinson's Maine Farmer's Almanac. In England *Old Moore's Almanac*,
first published in 1697 as a broadsheet by Dr Francis Moore, astrologer
and physician, remains a household name, and always includes favourable lunar planting and harvesting times.

'... CONSULT THE MOON'

Moon phase planting lore is bolstered on the one hand with im-
mutabilities and shot through on the other with personal fancies and
misunderstandings, as is inevitable in superstitions passed orally through
many generations. Moon beliefs may be traced for thousands of years:

the Greeks and Romans believed that sap in plants waxed and waned in monthly unison with the moon and, almost identically, in England, in *The Discoverie of Witchcraft* (1584) Reginald Scot wrote: 'The poor husbandman perceiveth that the increase of the moon maketh plants fruitful so as in the fulle moon they are in best strength, decaying in the wane and in the conjunction do entirely wither and fade.'

One doctrine appearing consistently in North America and Britain is that, by imitative magic, moon growth stimulates plant growth and that seeds sown or plants set during the growing moon will emulate her. Some advocate planting in the days immediately *preceding* the new moon so that seeds will have germinated and will be ready to grow as the moon begins to wax. Thomas Tusser, farmer-writer of the Elizabethan period, believed this and wrote:

> Sow peasen and beans in the wane of the moon,
> Who soweth them sooner he soweth too soone,
> That they with the planet may rest and arise,
> And flourish with bearing most plentiful wise.

Variants are many.

There are countless testimonies from all sorts and conditions of gardeners who follow these precepts. Mrs Gosling writes from Hawkchurch, Devon, 'Many of the older natives of this village firmly believe in "sowing by the moon",'[5] and Mrs E. E. Bowes states:

I am an East Anglian and well remember things my father used to say. He died recently at the age of ninety-two and was a wonderful gardener. Before he planted anything he would consult the calendar and the moon's phases. He told us that the moon had as much effect on soil as it had on tides, and would never plant anything until the moon was in its first quarter . . . saying 'Never plant too soon, consult the moon'.[6]

During his career as a professional gardener, E. Kidd worked as an 'improver' in the gardens of Thorpe Perrow, Yorkshire, noted for meticulous methods and discipline, in an atmosphere far removed from superstition. Yet there too it was customary for all seeds to be sown forty-eight hours before full moon.[7] H. J. Baker writes:

In 1937 my wife and I lived at Minehead Road, Knowle, Bristol. I planted all my seeds within 48 hours of the *full* moon and the results were almost unbelievable. Potatoes were huge, runner beans prolific, lettuces and radishes some of the largest you could wish to see. Nearly every one of the 'shorthorn' carrots was the size of a parsnip; one parsnip grew to a length of 48 inches . . . if you should miss one full moon you wait for the next, as the seeds planted then will catch up with any planted between moons.[8]

G. B. Millington recalls of William Haycock, the well-known civic gardener and foreman in the City of Birmingham Parks Department, Warwickshire: 'He often expressed the view that he would never plant seed when the moon was waning: in his experience the resulting crop was poor.'[9] 'Plant just before the moon is full and the moon's glow will speed the plant in its growth,' write Mr and Mrs W. C. Schempp of Riceville, Iowa.

Scientific investigation over the past fifty years seems to support these beliefs. The effects of the moon on plant growth, particularly illuminating to those working with Rudolf Steiner's agricultural indications, were examined by Dr L. Kolisko at the Biological Institute, Stuttgart, Germany, in the 1920s and 1930s, and the results published in *The Moon and the Growth of Plants* (1936).

While this is by no means the most recent research, it is interesting to look more closely at its findings, which firmly support those favouring planting forty-eight hours before full moon. Rain was found to be vital to the moon's ability to 'work into the plants'; in dry soil moon forces are ineffective, in accord with Dr Steiner's emphasis that lunar effects must be sought in the earth's fluids. It is worth remembering the persistent traditional links between the moon and the weather, particularly with rainfall.

Maize sown two days *before* full moon broke through the soil very quickly but to everyone's surprise seed sown two days later, *at* full moon, did not appear until the eighth day. Two days' difference in sowing produced eight days' retardation in germination and although it was assumed that this difference would vanish within a few weeks it instead became more apparent. Visitors to the experimental plots were rightly impressed, seeing on the one hand high and handsome plants sown before full, standing four feet tall, while the rest, two days younger, averaged only two and a half feet. This relationship was to persist throughout the plants' lifetime. The researchers concluded that for a plant to be exposed to the maximum forces flowing to earth at full moon, planting must be not *at* full moon, but rather earlier. To delay until the actual day of full moon exposed the germination process to already diminishing forces. The moon seemed to instil its powers into the plant at germination with effects decisive for the whole period of flowering and fruiting.

Lettuces and cabbages, sown two days before full moon and two days before new, were pricked out and transplanted at the same phases. At harvest time the younger 'full-moon plants', three times heavier, had firmer heads and yielded from 30 to 40 per cent more than the loosely built 'new-moon plants'. Over a five-year test period peas planted two days before full moon gave from 70 to 100 per cent better yields. New-moon peas withered and yellowed earlier. Full-moon tomatoes showed better yields by at least 60 per cent over new-moon plants. Dr Kolisko wrote: 'From the experiments of many years we can recommend with good conscience that tomatoes should be sown two days before Full Moon.'

The Italian scientist Girolamo Azzi has linked day-length with plant growth. His conclusions would suggest that while actual photosynthesis ceases on moonlight nights the lambent lunar glow, artificially prolonging the day, may encourage plants to 'tick over' rather than cease life processes as they do on dark nights: thus plants coming to full growth on moonlight nights and seeds sown then would have an edge on others.[10]

ABOVE- AND BELOW-GROUND CROPS

Along with general confidence in the waxing moon as a stimulant (which in other connections makes hair grow, bread rise and pork swell in the pot) are axioms concerned with specific vegetables. These are so contradictory as to further confuse an already obscure field, although some order can be brought to them.

An embracive belief from Kentucky to Maryland, Iowa to North Carolina and Nova Scotia, Britain, Germany and other parts of Europe—and particularly beloved of almanac compilers—is that vegetables bearing crops below ground (potatoes, carrots and parsnips) should be planted at the moon's dark; those fruiting above ground (cabbages, peas or beans) in the light. The rules apply equally to less familiar crops: in the Pacific Islands sugar cane, babasies and nut palms are planted at the new moon; yams, manioc, taro and other roots, in the dark: white planters and agricultural officers confirm that to ignore these rules produces inferior crops. 'You can start potatoes side by side, some planted in the dark of the moon, and some in the light, and those planted in the dark will be the best ever,' said an American gardener from the South. (It is this belief which partially controls Good Friday potato planting, as will be shown in Chapter 3.) Potatoes set in the decrease are less disposed to waste energy rising leafily from the soil and 'blooming themselves to death' in response to the moon's notorious powers of attraction; they will concentrate on tubers. 'Farmer Ben's Theory', a popular poem of nineteenth-century American farming magazines, put it thus:

> . . . *But potatoes now, are a different thing,*
> *They want to grow* down, *that is plain,*
> *But don't ye see, you must plant for that,*
> *When the moon is on the wane!*

One Nova Scotia gardener recklessly planted potatoes on the new moon and, although neighbours noticed splendid blossoms, the potatoes were only the size of peas when dug.[11] Of tomatoes ('above-ground crops') Mrs A. Elliott of Norwich writes:

My husband, Jonathan Elliott, worked as a horticulturalist for Williams and Belfield of Stalham and Catfield for over forty years, and he swears that his success in early tomato growing was due to the time the seeds were planted. Seeds planted with the first rising moon in November fruit two weeks before others planted in the wane, even if the first rising moon is later in the month than the waning one.[12]

But, as often in folklore, there may be virtue in defying precepts. American gardeners believe that potatoes planted in moonlight (against the rules) will show smooth, pallid skins, luminescent as the moon herself. In Maryland and Illinois, lettuces planted at the increase (as by the rules they should be) will 'run to seed'; and Mrs Keel of Chew Stoke, Somerset, writes: 'My father always sowed his cabbages for spring cutting on a *waning* moon; this, he said, stopped plants from "bolting". All other seeds he sowed with a growing moon.'[13]

In this confusion of instructions it is something of a relief to remember that the Kolisko experiments showed clearly that sowing forty-eight hours before full moon was as helpful to roots as to other crops. Carrots sown then were smooth and full coloured while new-moon carrots turned out shrivelled and pale; full-moon carrots were juicier, mild and sweet but new-moon carrots astringent, bitter and dry. Mrs Magda Jones of Broomfield, Essex, describes an interesting African experience: she mentions no specific planting point during the moon's growth, but results suggest that planting must have taken place shortly before full:

> We were living in Tanganyika Territory in East Africa in a Highland district, near Mbulu, about 100 miles from Arusha. Fresh vegetables were very scarce but I made a large vegetable garden on virgin soil near a small stream and could provide for my own and three other families . . . There were a few keen gardeners around including a friend of Czechoslovakian descent. He advised me never to sow carrots when the moon was in the descent, but rather to plant them after the new moon. I tried this out. From one packet of carrot seed I planted half the seeds on a descending moon and the other half on the ascending moon. Conditions of soil and daily watering were exactly the same. The first batch of seeds grew into badly formed, poor quality carrots; the other half, in less time, into beautiful carrots.[14]

Of a convincing personal experience on a Norfolk farm, Arthur Webster writes:

> This was at Church Lane, at Stow Bedon, Norfolk, in 1955, at the April moon. There is a 15-acre field: I drilled 7½ acres of peas two days before the moon came full and by the time the moon was full them peas had shoots on them one inch long! The other 7½ acres I drilled two days after the moon was full and they laid in the ground for nearly a month and never even swelled. They peas waited for the moon to come round again and them four days in sowing made a month's difference in cutting them.[16]

As a special bonus, peas and beans planted at the increase are certain to climb their sticks, drawn aloft by the moon's magnetic light: planted in the wane they cling to the ground.[10] A Buckinghamshire woodman provides another hint: 'You'll never get peas to climb up last year's sticks. If some of the sticks are this year's, and some last year's, they'll make for the new sticks. Beans don't mind at all.'

'My late father, Richard Dockett, was a great believer in planting vegetables and farm crops in a growing moon, particularly peas, broad beans and runner beans,' writes a Devon correspondent.[17] And in the Sea Islands of Georgia, just before full moon is mandatory for pea planting lest pods fail to swell: maximum size of the moon at full emblematizes maximum yield among vegetables. In the Hervey

Islands coconuts are always planted at full moon, so that the fruits to come will be of lunar dimensions and pearly whiteness.

A final influence is the position of the moon's horns. Around Boston lima beans are planted with the seed crescent lying parallel to the moon's crescent, to link the seed, visually and beneficially, with the moon. Pennsylvanian Germans, outstandingly successful farmers, adjure that peas, beans, corn and upward-growing vegetables be planted when the moon lies on her back, horns pointing upwards, and thus be stimulated by sympathetic magic to imitate in growth the upward thrust of the horns. If the horns point down at planting time leafy vegetables remain low and stunted. This school believes that potatoes, carrots and turnips *must* be sown when the horns point downwards to encourage downward activity and vigorous roots.[18] In North Carolina onion sets planted when the horns are up-pointing hoist themselves from the ground and lie unproductively on the surface.[19]

THE MOON AND FLOWERS

The vast concentration of moon planting lore in the vegetable garden points to origins in a time when the winning of food crops overshadowed all other considerations. The moon planter gives only a cursory glance to the flower garden. In the United States it is said that asters and any plants which gardeners wish to bear double flowers should be sown in the moon's light: all transplanting should be done then. A correspondent from Norfolk believes that 'flowers get ready to come out in full bloom during the time of moonlight', and in New England cuttings of houseplants are set at the August new moon, considered to be the best time for them to 'take'.[20] But these are the only fragments relating flower gardening to moon phase; that the link is so tenuous is clearly no accident but a pointer to the antiquity of the beliefs.

PLANTING, GRAFTING AND PRUNING FRUIT-TREES

'If you plant according to the course of the moon the tree will profit by it, and the fruit will come earlier,' advised a Guernsey gardener. Thomas Andros, in a manuscript of 1589 now in the Priaulx Library, Guernsey. He provided gardening advice in the Elizabethan manner,

Seventeenth-century additions, perhaps by the hand of Andros's son Charles, eventual Lieutenant-Bailiff of Guernsey, include: 'The nearer you approach the end and finish of the moon to plant, so much more beautiful in growth will the tree be, and the more fertile and fruitful; and if you plant at the new moon and its waxing, the trees, of a truth, will take better, and will take longer in producing their roots, wood and leaves, but they will be better at producing fruit than the others.' Then, with the hesitancy so redolent of the questioning seventeenth century, he adds: 'Nevertheless, this limitation to the seasons of the moon is not so certain that plants may not be as profitable as at other seasons of the moon . . .' Flexibility enough to solace gardeners of all persuasions! Directly echoing this old belief is the modern conviction that a tree planted in the new moon's light gives *more* fruit: one planted in the dark, *better* fruit.

Tree planting by the moon is well remembered. In February 1974, Viscount Scarsdale told the writer that over the past forty-five years he had often assisted his woodmen in planting some of the thousands of trees on his estate at Kedleston, Derbyshire, which covers eight square miles: 'When I plant trees in the waxing moon I think that they root down and grow bigger than trees planted in the waning moon. With a waxing moon and the leaves falling, it's just the right time to plant.' Kedleston has long been known for the beauty of its trees, hardwoods such as the oaks and sweet chestnuts planted between 1730 and 1770, accompanied by daffodils which are now growing wild.[21]

> *From moon being changed, till past be the prime,*
> *For graffing and cropping is very good time,*

wrote Tusser in 1580 (prime is the first three days following the new moon). The rule is as ancient as the Romans, and it hangs on. In the Ozarks every schoolchild is taught the unwisdom of touching fruit trees except at the moon's light. '*Faut tousiours enter en croissant de la lune,*' wrote Andros: 'One must always graft at the waxing of the moon.'[22] In North Carolina grapevines are trimmed just before full— this done, no birds or worms will attack them—and moonlight has also a hygienic, purificatory quality. It is believed that to trim trees at the moon's wane, when sap is down and vitality low, causes rot but branches pruned at the waxing are magically drawn outwards by the moon's 'pull': 'I am convinced that trees pollarded on the grow of the moon produce straighter rods—especially willows,' writes F. W. Baty of Longhope, Gloucestershire.

HARVESTING THE CROP

Tree-planting may bring a refreshing semblance of unanimity to moon lore, but it is a short-lived accord. With harvesting we are once again caught in the contradictory web:

> *The moone in the wane,*
> *Gather fruit for to last,*

says Tusser. 'It is a very common custom among the farmers and peasantry of Devonshire,' added a Victorian commentator, 'to gather in the "hoard fruit" in the "shrinking of the moon . . ."' apples then bruised in the gathering-in, do not decay afterwards,' a belief shared and practised by many gardeners on both sides of the Atlantic. The Romans, too, were convinced that fruit picked at a waning moon had the finest flavour.

Maryland farmers believe that crops ripen under moonlight rather than during dark nights. Maturity flows from growth; ripeness and rot from maturity. Moonbeams project a crop along the road to decay as surely as towards ripeness and it is therefore ill-advised to harvest seed or 'store' potatoes on moonlight nights, although digging the crop then provides the maximum number of potatoes for immediate use. (The moon magically increases the bulk of vegetables: as she grows smaller in the sky so do sap and substance diminish.[23]) The practice of storing nuts, grain and other foods in underground pits, safely protected from the moon's disruptive rays, is found from the Stone Age onwards and sprang from this concept of the moon's powers. In the tropics and sub-tropics this view was propounded by such sober-minded observers as naval officers, at least as late as the mid-nineteenth century: 'When I lived in Bermuda,' wrote one in 1851, 'if meat was exposed to the rays of the moon, it putrefied immediately,' a remarkable observation to receive confirmation in 1903 from the unlikely source of a report of the United States Weather

Bureau (Department of Agriculture), which had observed similar phenomena.

As might be expected, however, ranged against these solid traditions are others, flatly contradictory. One North Carolina faction believes that apples gathered in the *new* moon keep best, reflecting in longevity the span the moon is to enjoy,[24] and in harmony with the growth doctrine Cornish gardeners said that fruit picked at the waxing or full moon would keep its plumpness and would never 'shrump up'.[25]

Many gardeners still insist that essential oils are most concentrated in herbs picked when the moon is full. For example, Christopher Sansom of Kennel Moor, Godalming, Surrey, told the writer: 'Our old gardener, who retired in 1955, used to believe that horseradish would have the keenest tang if it were dug at the time of the full moon.'[26]

WEEDS AND LAWNS: FENCES AND FERTILIZERS

It is pleasant to find that the moon co-operates in the conflict with weeds. Plant vitality is lowest when the moon is in her fourth quarter and weeds pulled then will have no strength to sprout again. Briar and brushwood die from the roots if cut at the old moon, time of minimum growth; for full effectiveness unwanted trees are disposed of at the May moon's dark: in Iowa the dark of the August moon is the proper time to tackle box elder.[27] But it must be conceded that another school firmly favours destruction at the very moment of *full* moon; then, according to the doctrine of the ancients, the plant is struck down at its peak of vitality and its seeds, constrained by the arriving wane, will not germinate.

For lushest lawns with fewest weeds, sow grass seed in the moon's increase. Since moonlight encourages growth, mowing during waxing means that grass quickly needs attention again: lawn-mowing done at the dark lasts longest. Fence rails cut in moonlight are said to crimp, twist and decay faster than those cut in the less disturbing dark. Pig-farmers in the Ozarks turn this to advantage by building fences in the moon's last quarter when the bottom rails will sink into the ground and defeat the pigs' efforts to uproot them: fence posts set in the old moon settle 'like they took roots and growed'. Those cut in the August wane are reckoned by many rural Americans to last twice as long as others;

and even today some builders prefer not to shingle a house in the moon's waxing, lest the shingles be 'drawn up', nails spring out and boards warp in response to the mischief of moonlight.

Farmers have often remarked that post-holes dug in the decrease are readily refilled levelly with the earth removed from them: if the work is done in the growing moon, however, there will be far more earth than can possibly be replaced—in accord with the moon's enlarging influence. Cato, the Roman agriculturalist, advised that manures be spread at the wane or they would never sink into the soil as the gardener wished, but rather dry up and lie uselessly on the surface or even blow away. Like the ancient Romans the Pennsylvanian Germans require that for best results manures be applied with the moon's horns down-pointing to drive the fertilizer *down* into the earth.

GARDENING BY MOONLIGHT: THE WEATHER

Some gardeners solicit the moon's benignity personally and work by moonlight. In Illinois they say that fruit trees planted under the radiant new moon will always bear well.[28] The supposed warming 'heat' of the moon means that orchard-trees, particularly delicate peach-trees, coming into bloom on light nights will never be frosted: killing frosts are said never to occur during a waxing moon.

These beliefs spring from the notion that the moon, like the sun, generates heat. 'Trees which are planted in a row are warmed by the sun and the moon equally on all sides, with the result that more grapes and olives form, and that they ripen earlier,' wrote Varro about 36BC. Scientists add a mere scrap of support. Professor Charles Piazzi Smyth, the Astronomer Royal of Scotland, reported in 1857 that on a recent expedition to the peak of Teneriffe in the Canaries his thermometers were affected by the heat of the moon's rays, even at the lower of his two observation stations. But more recently, in *The Moon* (1960), Professor Zdenek Kopal of Manchester University observed that the actual amount of heat emitted by even the full moon is slight indeed: in fact barely sufficient to raise the temperature of a moon-bathed landscape by one thousandth of a degree.[29]

There seems greater justification for the school which links the moon's silvery radiance with frost. Richard Jefferies, the naturalist, found that country folk in Berkshire and Wiltshire affirmed that irrigated meadows and other open water would not freeze until the moon rose, its pearly gleam causing the water to 'catch' and spicules of ice to spread over the surface.[30] Magically moon-touched water reflects the sparkle of hoar frost. For this view there is reassurance from science: night temperature and lunar phase do appear to be linked. In North Wales Herbert Henstock noted a regular fall in the minimum night temperature for two or three nights about the time of full moon. Data from America, Canada, South Africa, Australia and India showed similar effects with variations ranging from 4 to 40°F, greater in summer but independent of latitude and height above sea level. Those relating moon to weather change ('The moon and the weather change together') are well served and are becoming better so. Sir Bernard Lovell (no ally of superstition) wrote in the London *Sunday Times*, 15 May 1964, of emerging links between moon phase, rainfall, magnetic storms and other phenomena '. . . almost . . . as though we are moving through a series of scientific fantasies to a proof of ancient beliefs'. In 1962 D. A. Bradley and M. A. Woodbury of New York University and Glenn W. Brier of the Massachusetts Institute of Technology correlated lunar phase and weather in the United States. It was concluded that the moon's phase could account for almost 65 per cent of the changes in United States rainfall. Australian scientists produced similar figures.[31]

THE SUN'S PATH

The old sun god, *Sol Invictus*, the Unconquerable Sun, source of the world's visible beauty, rules the garden year. If the moon is queen by night, the sun is king by day. Until midsummer the sun's vigour stimulates; the solstice is the peak of summer and, after it, imitatively, under gentler suns, plant growth dies away.

The symbolism involved in the sun's effect upon seed laid in the ground is to a great extent phallic. Around Bayeux, Normandy, sowing must be done just as the sun's first brilliance falls on the garden on a spring morning. In Iowa, Kentucky and Illinois above-ground vegetables planted in the morning 'rise from the ground with the rising sun'; below-ground vegetables, bulbs and flower tubers such as dahlias, planted in the afternoon, 'sink down with it'. Another school specifies morning planting for all vegetables, citing *Ecclesiastes xi*. 6: 'In the morning sow thy seed...' 'My mother always said that they would grow with the day if planted in the morning; in the afternoon they would go down with the night,' remembers an Adams County, Illinois, gardener. In Staffordshire a hundred years ago care was taken to cut grass in the morning if growth were desired; in the afternoon if not. The sun's diurnal sweep across the heavens is an important measure and the apex of noon significant: 'Set cabbages in the middle of the day,' advised the *Old Farmer's Almanac* in 1805. Even today in the Ozarks it is commonly said that any tree may be transplanted with perfect safety at any time of year provided that the work is done at noon precisely and that the tree is watered at noon each day until natural rain falls.

Biodynamic research has provided some support for these traditions. Recent German experiments revealed a daily plant rhythm: sap rose in the morning; then about midday the plants seemed to be still and 'marking time'. With the dying afternoon light, activity declined, and as evening approached the plants clung more firmly to earth.[32]

BOUNDARIES OF TIME

In the ancient Celtic world the boundaries of time periods—night and day, month and month, summer and winter—were thought to be haunted by mysterious powers with a propensity for, at once, good and evil. The veils between the supernatural and real worlds were then thin, fairies were about and witches worked their woe. Certain acts were taboo at these fateful moments. Shadows linger. In Illinois it is still said that seed planted on the thirty-first day of any month comes to nothing and that to dig or to gather crops after nightfall brings sickness or death to the gardener. As late as 1890 no green plant was ever carried into a Derbyshire house after sunset, or disaster would surely strike: forces of special menace walked abroad at nightfall.

But if the maleficent is dreaded, the accompanying beneficent aspect of the supernatural may be courted. Potatoes dug after sunset are sweeter and will never rot, and a correspondent born in Caernarvonshire, Wales, in 1898, reports 'a strong local belief there that an apple tree planted after dark would be sure to take'.[33]

'THE SUN LEAVES HIS SEAT'

Even to the twentieth-century mind an eclipse of the sun is an awe-inspiring—even sinister—event: an unnatural silence settles over the day, the sky grows coppery dark, birds cease to sing. To early man an eclipse, when the new moon passes in front of the sun, was a time of infinite dread when the 'sun left his seat' and evil was unrestrained. It was an ill moment indeed for garden work or crops: 'Neither graft, set, sow, or plant anything that day whereon there happeneth to be an eclipse, either of sun or moon,' was the uncompromising verdict of the sixteenth century.[34] Today Pennsylvanian German gardeners still say that should a solar eclipse occur when the sweet corn is in blossom, the ears will never fill. Mrs Evelyne E. Bowes adds an experience of her father's:

> When he was a young man he was gardener to a titled lady who was very fond of Parma violets and it was my father's job to see that she had two or three bunches each week. I can well remember seeing four large glass frames full of these beautiful violets. On one occasion my father was planting two of the frames with new plants. He had finished one and was planting the other during an eclipse of the sun. None of the plants put in during the eclipse grew. They remained stunted and were finally pulled out and burned. There is an old East Anglian saying that 'everything in the garden stands still during an eclipse' [35]

Here too must be mentioned 'day of the week planting', still something of a force in both America and Britain, if now only meaningful to the older generation of gardeners. In the past many, connecting the day calamitously with the crucifixion, avoided Friday planting. Fruit picked on a Sunday was said to return to the tree as fast as the picker could remove it. Sunday work in the garden is still taboo in many rural areas and it is sometimes said that nothing planted then will thrive. In Ireland herbs pulled on a Sunday are savourless and useless, particularly for medicinal purposes. Mrs M. Myers writes of a Lancashire and West Riding of Yorkshire tradition that 'you may *give* away anything out of your garden on a Sunday, but if you *sell* your produce your crops will fail that season', a tradition to be found in North America also. Until recently the prohibition on Sunday garden work was taken very seriously indeed: for example, the flower show schedule of the Surrey village of Ashstead in 1900 specifically barred from entry any gardener who worked in his garden on a Sunday, although there was a dispensation for 'watering and tending'.

Cecil Atkins remembers the rules governing work on the rectory allotments at Waddesdon, Buckinghamshire, earlier this century, which (although the rector was nominally in charge) suggest that the allotment-holders were also required to revere tacitly the Earth Mother. Occupiers must cultivate by 'spade husbandry' alone (the Goddess exacts the sweat of her followers); the same crop must not be grown on the same land for two successive years. Each occupier, in each year of his occupancy, must spread upon his land—'in a workman-like manner'—'three good loads of dung' to each rood (the ritual sacrifice to keep land in good heart). Work on the day of the sun-god was naturally forbidden. Drunkenness, fighting or gambling exposed the tenant to the forfeiture of his plot—the instinctive uneasy conviction that violence and immorality imperil the earth's fertility is old as time. Until fifty years ago 'rough music'—mob harassment with the beating of pots and pans and the shouting of insults—often greeted infringers of the village code of morals: victims seldom recovered their honour and often, to everyone's satisfaction, fled the neighbourhood. Immoral behaviour slighted the earth and brought retribution from Nature, and crop failures in its wake.

NORTH TO SOUTH: EAST TO WEST

The Pole Star, North's guardian, stands for constancy in the wheeling heavens. In Cambridgeshire, in the last century, gardeners planted parsley in gardens lighted by spring starlight, with drills running from north to south, as established by the Pole Star.

North-to-south planting, connected with the earth's magnetic field, is superstitiously said by practitioners to benefit crops. It is well remembered. Mrs A. F. Smith of Patchway, Bristol, writes that her father always set kidney beans in rows on this orientation[36] and 'One Hertfordshire man aligned his rows of seeds to the points of the compass and this made his allotment look a little out of the ordinary as he had diagonal rows of peas and other vegetables running from north to south.'[37] A Toronto photographer, Gilbert Milne, digs the trench to hold his tomato plants on a north-south orientation and sets young plants with roots gathered and pointing north. From his garden tomatoes weighing 3½ pounds are by no means uncommon.[38] There are of course many rationalizations: 'If you sow from east to west, rain and wind come down the rows and knock plants over,'[39] and 'Have rows running north to south and plants get equal amounts of sun on either side.'

In the nineteenth century transition from colder to warmer climates was deemed essential for the production of quality seed potatoes, and Scotch seed was invariably preferred to English. In Ulster gardeners still say with conviction that seed should *never* be brought from southern Ireland, even from a more southerly point in the province.[40] But climate has in fact been shown to have little influence, and healthy seed potatoes grow as well in southern England as in northern Scotland. The belief may therefore be merely a recollection of ancient deference to the south as a dreaded source of warmth and therefore of disease; diseases brought to England by traders spread northwards from southern ports. Tudor houses in particular were sometimes built lacking south-facing windows or doors for, however inviting the prospect, owners, with justification, preferred the safer colder northern view. But is dread of disease the only reason for favouring northern seed (the belief is lively yet)? Might it not be a further example of primitive respect for the mystery of the earth's magnetic field?

Compass-points have played a role in tree-planting since Roman times. Dryden's translation of Virgil's second *Georgic* speaks of:

> *Some peasants, not t'omit the nicest care,*
> *Of the same soil their nursery prepare,*
> *With that of their plantations; lest the tree,*
> *Translated, should not with the soil agree.*
> *Beside, to plant it as it was, they mark*
> *The heaven's four quarters on the tender bark,*
> *And to the north or south restore the side,*
> *Which at their birth did heat or cold abide . . .*

In 1802 that standby, *The Old Farmer's Almanac*, concurred: 'Be sure to set that side south which was south before, because it cannot endure the cold,' thus perpetuating a belief with a pedigree of at least 2,000 years. In the seventeenth century, too, Sir Thomas Browne insisted that at grafting time the south-facing part of fruit-tree buds or scions be inserted into the south side of the stock, or they would not take.

The traditional orientations—half magic, half commonsense—have attracted recent scientific interest. Dr Urban J. Pittman, an agronomist with the Agricultural Research Station, Lethbridge, Alberta, Canada, found that across North America the roots of cereals and certain weeds consistently aligned themselves on a north-south axis and that the germination of some cereals was accelerated if their long axes and embryo ends were oriented towards the north magnetic pole. Dr Pittman has suggested that when old gardeners insisted that pumpkin and other seeds be planted 'pointing north', they may well have been right. He has made further investigations into plant response. If, prior to planting, certain grains are passed through a magnetic field they are found to germinate faster, to produce 5–15 per cent higher yields and to mature earlier. Several enterprising manufacturers are marketing devices incorporating magnets over which seed passes on its way through the seed-drill. About 1960 two Russian scientists, A. V. Krylock and G. A. Tarakanova, showed too that tomatoes ripen faster nearer to the south than to the north pole of a magnet, although they could offer no explanation. Eventually such investigations may reveal the full truth of the old superstitions.

East-to-west orientation recalls sun-worship and the 'sunwise turn' of mythology. Christian churches are built on this orientation, wedding parties went to church 'with the sun' for security against evil spirits, and millstones were set to run sunwise. Today many stirrers of jam find themselves following the old turn and it is no surprise to learn that tradition demands that hedge trimming and garden cultivation be done from east to west in salute to Sol.

Here brief mention must also be made of electroculture and similar doctrines, seemingly very modern but in fact linked with the folklore of electricity and the earth's electromagnetic field. Many gardeners respect such practices. Henry Pfau, aged seventy-six, formerly of Camden, New Jersey, and now retired and living in Citrus Springs, Florida, credits electroculture with producing outstanding vegetables from his 400-ft square garden. He sets poles round the edges of the garden, strings copper wire between them and runs another set of insulated bell wires to the roots of young tomato plants. Mr Pfau believes that atmospheric charges pass through the wires into the soil to produce the choice 'tender-tasting vegetables for a giant' which he so much enjoys. His Japanese radishes weigh 3–4 pounds each (a good but not remarkable weight; depending upon variety these giant radishes can weigh up to 30 pounds each, and may be stored like turnips). Tomatoes—of the 'beefsteak' variety—ripen at 3½ pounds. Mr Pfau agrees that science has not yet proved that these procedures do produce bigger and better vegetables but he is, nevertheless, a firm believer: 'I have seen it happen with my own eyes.'

Gilbert Milne, who also believes in oriented planting, uses metals and pyramidal culture as an energy source. Wire rods form pyramids with the proportions of the Great Pyramid of Cheops. Precise angles are essential. Houseplants collected from display tables and windowsills are moved under the pyramids for the night and metal coathangers are tucked into the pots of outlying plants to link them to those directly under pyramids. Seedlings treated thus are said to grow more vigorously, and pests are eliminated. Mr Milne's plants may grow in metal cans rather than in traditional earthenware pots: others have metal nails embedded in their soil or pins pushed into their stems as growth aids (it is tempting to see a link with the practice of hammering nails into fruit trees, described elsewhere). Another Ontario gardener, Robert Gordon of Unionville, in 1975 gathered 97 tomatoes from one plant growing under a wire pyramid: yet another, Les Brown of Bancroft, grows crops in a 30-ft high pyramid-shaped greenhouse. Smaller pyramids are now marketed commercially, some, it is claimed, 'oriented to the true north'. The Cheops Pyramid Company of St Louis, Missouri, among others, offers pyramids on a ten-inch base at $7.00 and claims that they will 'generate bio-cosmic energy', 'stimulate plant growth' and 'sprout healthier seeds quicker'.

But despite the high testimonials of some users, scientists are sceptical. In February 1976 Professor Herman Tiessen said that experiments at the University of Guelph, Ontario, with wire frames said to follow the dimensions of the Great Pyramid and to collect 'positive ions, negative electrons, magnetic, polar and many other energies' produced no visible effect whatsoever on plants. It was claimed that pyramids favourably influenced germination, plant growth and the size, yield and colour of flowers, fruit and vegetables. Scientists at Guelph sowed twenty seeds each of lettuce, cauliflower, asparagus, tomato and muskmelon in twenty pots and placed them at random under pyramids of varying colours and materials. Nothing was noted; plants under pyramids looked exactly the same as untreated controls. Leaves were as green; plant vigour identical. Professor Tiessen suggested, however, that even the fact of the investigations might add weight to the belief—future pyramidologists would feel that the university was at least interested enough to investigate: 'Let us have it on record that our investigations failed to find any supportive evidence.'

Putative connections between electricity and plant growth have aroused curiosity for centuries. In 1746 in Edinburgh, Maimbray found that myrtle bushes set by an electrical conductor grew three-inch buds in winter. In France Abbé Bertholon, in *De L'Electricité des Végétaux*, described how his gardener, standing upon an insulating pad, watered vegetables from an electrified can. Treated lettuces grew to great size and the abbé suggested that the best plant fertilizer, electricity, might one day be found to come free from the sky in the form of lightning.

Thunderstorms in late July or early August 'ripen the crops'. Mrs M. Clarke of Grantham, in the *Daily Telegraph*, 25 July 1974, remembered staying with country cousins many years ago, seeing sheet lightning without rain or thunder and being given this old rustic explanation. According to E. L. Hawke, who in 1950 edited Inward's *Weather Lore* for the Royal Meteorological Society, there is scientific backing for this belief. Lightning in its passage through the air produces ammonia and nitrogen oxides; and ammonia dissolved in rain becomes ammonium hydroxide, a plant food. The nitrogen oxides react with atmospheric moisture to form nitric and nitrous acids which act as soluble nitrates and fertilize the soil. A thundery summer is thus an aid to crops, and the rain and heat associated with stormy weather is also helpful in bringing them to maturity.

Pursuing the theory that abundant plant growth takes place in the presence of electricity, a Finnish scientist, Selim Lemström, investigated the growth rings of fir-trees in Spitzbergen, North Norway and Lapland, during the years 1868–84 and found that high annual growth coincided with periods of intense sunspot and aurora borealis, or 'northern lights', activity. With overhead wires and metal rods set into the ground, Lemström linked flowers planted in metal pots with a static generator: after eight weeks plants receiving electricity showed weight gains of more than 50 per cent over untreated plants. The same techniques produced doubled yields of garden strawberries.

Lemström's theories were expounded in his book *Electricity in Horticulture* (1904). His findings attracted the interest of Sir Oliver Lodge, physicist and psychical researcher, who suspended a wire grid attached to insulators over his crops, creating an electromagnetic field. His yields of Red Fife wheat increased by 40 per cent; a collaborator achieved yield increases of 20 per cent in wheat and potatoes, vastly improved strawberry yields and fruit notable for succulence and sweetness.

These and other experiments, incomplete and inconclusive as they yet are, may come to add substance to ancient beliefs ascribing plant growth and crop maturing to the presence of electricity in its natural form.

SIGNS OF THE ZODIAC

Completing the trio of prime cosmic aids for the gardener is the zodiac, an imaginary zone some 16° wide encircling the heavens, in which lie the apparent paths of the sun, moon and principal planets. The Egyptians and Babylonians divided the zodiac into twelve equal parts, or 'signs', each named after the fixed star constellation which lay within it, and since all the signs except Libra were named after living things, the belt was called the zodiac or 'zone of animals'. In his first *Georgic* Virgil noted: 'Through twelve bright signs Apollo guides the year . . .' The zodiacal signs, most familiar today through newspaper horoscopes, quickly became related to fate, to medicine and the human body and to many activities such as fishing and gardening.

Every calendar month the sun passes through about two-thirds of one sign and one-third of the next. The moon, on the other hand, passes through *all* the signs within this time, dwelling in each sign for two or three days once (or sometimes twice) each month. Herein is said to rest the benefit to gardeners; the reputation of the moon sign governing each day of the month designates the day favourable or otherwise for gardening.

Six signs, the 'northern signs'—Aries, Taurus, Gemini, Cancer, Leo, Virgo—ascend on the northern side of the celestial equator, and six—Libra, Scorpio, Sagittarius, Capricornus, Aquarius, Pisces—descend on

c

the south side. All almanacs show in chart form the sun and moon signs governing each month and day of the year; the planet governing the signs; the parts of the body ruled by the signs; and associated elements—fire, air, water or earth.

It may be helpful to consider a particular month by way of example. April is ruled by the sun signs Aries (21 March–21 April) and Taurus (21 April–23 May). A well known North American almanac (based on Central Standard Time) gives the moon signs for 1976 for the month as follows:

1, 2	Taurus	16, 17	Sagittarius
3, 4, 5	Gemini	18, 19	Capricorn
6, 7	Cancer	20, 21, 22	Aquarius
8, 9	Leo	23, 24	Pisces
10, 11	Virgo	25, 26, 27	Aries
12, 13	Libra	28, 29	Taurus
14, 15	Scorpio	30	Gemini

PLANTING BY THE SIGNS

Planting rules turning on the signs of the zodiac, passed down devotedly through many generations, survive particularly stubbornly in the rural United States. There are a number of systems to follow—and rancorous arguments are likely between their followers. Researchers at Raburn Gap-Nacoochee School, Georgia, interviewed in recent years some thirty gardeners and farmers in that neighbourhood who follow the signs without question—or who scoff at them roundly. Their depositions present a revealing picture of believers and non-believers in one area of rural America today.[41] The doctrine of planting by the signs (even confirmed supporters admit that its adherents have fallen off somewhat in recent years) crossed to America with early settlers from Europe. In Germany, for example, astrology has always enjoyed popularity and similarly, in America, the Pennsylvanian Germans preserve much zodiacal lore. Instructions for British gardeners are slighter, except perhaps for those in works such as *The Husbandman's Practice, or, Prognostication for Ever* (1664):

> Set, sow seeds, graft and plant, the moone being in Taurus, Virgo, or in Capricorne ... graft in March at the moone's increase, she being in Taurus or Capricorne ...

SIGNS OF THE ZODIAC

SIGN	DATE OF SUN'S ENTRY	ASSOCIATED ELEMENT	PART OF BODY RULED	RULING PLANET	SYMBOL
Aries, the Ram	21 March	Fire	Head	Mars	♈
Taurus, the Bull	21 April	Earth	Neck	Venus	♉
Gemini, the Twins	23 May	Air	Shoulders, Arms	Mercury	♊
Cancer, the Crab	22 June	Water	Breast, Stomach	Moon	♋
Leo, the Lion	23 July	Fire	Heart	Sun	♌
Virgo, the Virgin	23 August	Earth	Bowels	Mercury	♍
Libra, the Scales	23 September	Air	Loins, Kidneys	Venus	♎
Scorpio, the Scorpion	23 October	Water	Genitals	Mars	♏
Sagittarius, the Archer	22 November	Fire	Thighs	Jupiter	♐
Capricornus, the Goat	23 December	Earth	Knees, Joints	Saturn	♑
Aquarius, the Watercarrier	21 January	Air	Legs	Uranus	♒
Pisces, the Fishes	20 February	Water	Feet	Neptune	♓

NB: This chart shows sun signs only. Moon signs change every few days, and for them a current almanac should be consulted

Many modern practitioners claim biblical support, particularly from *Genesis i.* 14:

> ... let there be lights in the firmament of the heaven to divide the day from the night; and let them be for signs, and for seasons, and for days, and years ...

and *Ecclesiastes iii.* 1-2:

> To everything there is a season, and a time to every purpose under the heaven ... a time to plant, and a time to pluck up that which is planted ...

There are strong religious overtones to many instructions and a comfortably pious feeling that the whole doctrine enjoys the approval of heaven.

Before the start of the spring gardening season the thoughtful gardener makes his plans, his almanac open before him, choosing days in proper signs for sowing seeds and performing other garden work. Some are pleased if they can combine the correct zodiacal sign with a favourable phase of the moon. A gardener who ignores 'fruitful days' and does not trouble to plant on them never gathers more than mediocre crops, say believers: some systems require planting to the very hour, however inconvenient. Margaret and Richard Norton, highly successful gardeners of Betty's Creek, told the Raburn Gap interviewers that they had planted strictly by the signs for over ten years and felt the doctrine to be perfectly reliable. Anyone who once began to use it would never give it up, they said. Since there are fourteen good planting days in the month it was possible that even non-believers might hit upon a good day sometimes, but they would enjoy nothing like the consistent successes anticipated by those who paid proper attention to the signs: but some common sense was required: a correct lunar position could not compensate for poor weather conditions or low temperatures.

Signs planting is most usually a matter for unquestioning faith, but in Germany underlying reasons for its success have been sought by bio-dynamic gardeners. In his *Agricultural Course* Rudolf Steiner showed definite ways in which plant life develops under planetary influences. Franz Rulni and Heinrich Schmidt, working with Steiner's principles, have drawn up a sowing calendar with special attention to the moon's phases, its nodes, conjunctions, nearness to earth and waxing and waning. Following these indications, Maria Thun carried out nine years' research with annual plants. In simple terms it may be said that she found plants to be four-fold beings, displaying strongest root, leaf, flower or fruit development according to the position at planting time of the moon in the zodiacal constellations. Roots developed best in plants sown when the moon was in Taurus, Virgo and Capricorn (earth forces); leaves in Pisces, Cancer or Scorpio (water forces); fruit in Aries, Leo or Sagittarius (fire forces). The moon acted as mediator between the fixed stars and the elemental formative activity of plants. These findings, although apparently contradicting some traditions (Virgo, for example, does not emerge as a flower stimulator), are clearly of great interest to those who practise signs planting.[42]

T. E. BLACK'S SYSTEM

Typifying the traditional American 'signs' gardener and small farmer is T. E. Black of Andalusia, Alabama, who tells us that he was born in Pike County in 1894 and who publishes a 'planting by the signs' guide entitled *God's Way*.[43] The system has been tested for over twenty years and Mr Black is so confident of the book's practical value that he writes: 'One hill of tomatoes will pay for it.'

God's Way offers best and second-best dates based on the governing moon sign for planting root crops, above-ground crops (including corn, tobacco, watermelons, tomatoes, collards, cabbages, peppers, okra, peas, squash and cucumbers) and for transplanting flowers and fruit-trees. For long life, Mr Black advises that vase and bouquet flowers be cut during water or earth signs. Flowers planted in the proper sign will produce abundant blooms and will stay green in dry weather. Sweet and 'Irish' potatoes (the familiar *Solanum tuberosum*), bell peppers, egg plant and tomatoes, planted in a favourable sign, produce yields three to five times greater than usual and, while cucumbers incorrectly planted will readily dry out or grow crookedly, those linked by planting with the proper moon sign will be thick on the vine, even in poor seasons, straight, comely and marketable. Proper observance of harvesting dates affects the keeping qualities of crops: seed saved from plants sown in an unpropitious sign produces steadily deteriorating crops; seed properly saved doubles the harvest, says Mr Black.

In each twenty-eight-day period there are fourteen good planting days; while seven are fairly satisfactory, although plants sown in them tend to suffer during drought: of the remaining days, two are unfavourable and cause seed to rot, two are poor and produce only a partial crop, and three are quite hopeless for planting. Margins are slim and the gardener must waste no time: it is prudent to make preparations a day ahead of the sign, so that all may be ready for sowing on the exact day (or at the exact time). The cover of *God's Way* bears impressive photographs of okra plants: one, planted in a fruitful sign, bearing many pods; the other, set in an unproductive sign, rich in leaf only. 'Same land, same work,' declares Mr Black: 'People have just been sleeping over the signs for the past fifty years, but they are fast waking up to them again.' He believes that gardeners should ignore the moon's phases as planting guides; to plant on a growing moon may give slightly larger stalks and vines, but little more: 'The signs are what counts.'

Gardeners following a system like *God's Way* are often content to rely on the almanac, to check the sign for the day and to go ahead with plantings, without investigating further. But some believers, relying less on blind faith, like to explore more closely the reasons why certain signs favour, or do not favour, particular crops. Much turns on the doctrine of imitative magic. The subject is very wide but some of the most generally accepted indicators are as follows:

'Up' or northern signs obviously favour climbing vegetables: lima beans planted in 'down' or southern signs, for example, will refuse to climb their poles at all, while onions set in 'up' signs jump from the ground and require replanting. Shrubs root well if planted in 'down' signs, trees best in water or earth signs. Little or nothing should be sown in fiery, barren signs (excellent though these are for destroying undergrowth by burning and for clearing land). Grafting should never be done on a Sunday—in no way for religious reasons but because it is the hot, dry sun's day when grafts are likely to fail.

Links between the human body and the zodiac come strongly into play. *Aries*, the Ram, which governs the head, favours the growth of vegetables of head-like shape (cabbages, turnips and swedes) although, as a fire sign, it is poor for seed-sowing, except for hot herbs ruled by Mars, such as onions and tobacco. As a dry sign it favours preparation of fine, dry tilths.

Planting under *Taurus* the Bull, symbol of red blood, will encourage the growth of dark-red beets with fortitude to withstand drought. As an earth sign Taurus is first-class for all roots, especially peanuts and potatoes, and is second-best for all above-ground vegetables and for flowers.

Gemini, the Twins, especially the 'Twin Days' of March, April and May, aids garden-making. All crops, such as beans, peas, melons and cucumbers, for which multiplication—in the manner of twins—is especially desired should be sown in Gemini when two blossoms for one are to be expected. Pennsylvanian Germans believe that Gemini's peas will be consistently double-podded.

Cancer, a water and 'growing' sign, is most favoured of all signs for plantings and transplantings and is excellent for the preparation of potato- and seed-beds.

Leo the Lion, as a fire sign, anatomically 'in the heart' and therefore of a fundamentally stimulating effect, strengthens plants (as do those sturdy beasts the Ram and the Bull). The Lion's governance of the heart can be used destructively, as a 'death sign', and is propitious for weeding lawns and 'deading brushwood' for lasting results. Neither weeds nor undergrowth cut then are likely to rise again. It is said that an axe struck into a sapling in Leo will cause the tree to wither in a few hours and to be quite dead in three months. Ruled by the sun, Leo is beneficial for cultivation but poor for plantings. Sweetcorn planted in Leo shows typical characteristics: a hard round stalk, depleted ears and a propensity to wither during drought.

Seeds sown during *Virgo*, the Virgin, Posy Girl, or Flower Woman (she holds a sprig of blossom), produce flowers, rather than fruit. Virgo's days are called 'Bloom Days'; if challenged, practitioners brush aside as a mere peccadillo the need for flowers to precede fruit! One old lady, contemptuously fingering stunted beans at a roadside vegetable stand near Memphis, last summer, murmured 'They must have been planted when the maid held the posies!' Virgo corn will 'mature green'—a valueless crop. Squash, tomatoes and cucumbers thus misplanted will have fine 'false' blossoms but few fruits. However, Virgo aids such activities as seeding lawns, sowing grass and clearing ground for planting.

Libra, the Scales or Balance, is a 'growing' sign, particularly favourable to zinnias through the analogy of scale-like zinnia petals. All flowers and above-ground crops sown at this sign do well.

Fruitful *Scorpio*, the Scorpion, rules the loins, the seat of fertility, and there is no better sign in which to marry! Scorpio ranks second only to Cancer in general merit, and some say it is best of all for above-ground crops and second-best for roots. Many Ozark farmers choose Scorpio for corn planting and setting fruit-trees; and (for obvious magical reasons) it has a high reputation for the sowing of cucumbers!

Sagittarius, the Archer, encourages growing plants to 'shoot up' and to go to seed, but emerges as the most profitable of all the fire signs and effective for the sowing of hot onions. Since it is a dry sign it favours soil cultivation, but is ill-favoured for transplanting.

Capricornus, the Goat, an earth sign, favours onions, beets, potatoes, peanuts, turnips, parsnips and other roots and is the second-best choice for flowers, above-ground crops and transplanting. It is excellent for pruning, and trees trimmed in it bleed less. As a dry earth sign it favours the harvesting of 'hoard fruit' and indeed most crops.

Vegetables sown in *Aquarius*, the Watercarrier, may turn out to be 'watery' and lacking in substance, but nevertheless the sign ('in the legs') produces straight smooth parsnips and carrots. Potatoes should never be dug in a moist sign lest they become soft and sprout.

Pisces, the Fishes, another moist 'growing' sign, resembles Cancer in influence, smiles on all crops, bulbs and flowers, and, in December and January, on the pruning and planting of fruit-trees, vines and shrubs. Pisces vegetables will be tender, crisp and prolific but 'one should avoid planting potatoes "in the feet" lest they be covered with small knobbly toes'! In general however, despite this exclusion, roots harvested in Pisces (feet) or Capricornus (knees) will give greatest satisfaction to the gardeners.

PROS AND CONS

Although T. E. Black claims that in recent years 250,000 gardeners have followed his system alone—and there are of course many rival systems —it must be conceded that the numbers of those respectful of moon and signs in planting, pruning and garden work are a mere shadow of the army of believers of the fifteenth to nineteenth centuries. As with many beliefs, an end of wholesale credulity came about with the enquiring climate of the seventeenth century. In *La Maison Rustique* (1660) Richard Surflet included as a matter of course lists of seeds to be sown at new, full and old moons; but by 1662 John Evelyn in *Sylva* felt confident enough to roundly repudiate all moon humbug, and in 1706 Louis Liger pronounced emphatically in *The Retir'd Gardener* that after thirty years' observation of such superstitions he felt them 'no weightier than old wives' tales . . . graft in what time of the Moone you please; if your graft be good and graft on a good stock, provided you do it like an artist you will be sure to succeed . . .' and '. . . plant in any Quarter of the Moone, I'll answer for your success, the first or last day of the Moone being equally favourable'.

But, despite these denunciations, what is the position today? It took many generations to diminish the undoubted force of astrology in everyday life. Indeed some, reflecting upon horoscopes and zodiacal jewellery, might argue that its influence is still pervasive; it is certainly far from dead; the almanacs, highly successful commercial publications with wide sales, demonstrate that. In parts of the rural United States the moon and signs school of gardening is very assured indeed. In assessing the durability of astrological dogma one must bear in mind that there are those who believe and are unafraid to say so; those who laugh publicly and take care to practise privately; and those who preserve, without open comment, their parents' ways. There is a growing number of recent converts to moon and signs planting, largely among unconventional young people seeking new life-styles on remote homesteads and communes. Obviously many gardeners produce excellent crops without the slightest heed for traditional lore; but the superstitious also do well and, as far as 'planting by the signs' is concerned, are quick to point out the ease with which the non-believer can unwittingly strike good days for planting and thus claim a credit for science which they feel rightly belongs to the moon and zodiac.

Today there is too a growing sentiment even among orthodox scientists that superstitions and traditions should at least be examined before being consigned to the scrapheap. Research has at last begun to categorize the apparently undeniable cosmic influences at work on plant growth and weather. In the field of bio-magnetics, for example, a number of American scientists have shown how the earth's electro-magnetic fields, influenced by sun and moon, in turn affect all life. Frank A. Brown, Morrison Professor of Biology, Northwestern University, Illinois, in an experiment reported in the *Biological Bulletin* in 1973, immersed baskets of beans in water and, over a long period, weighed them each day at noon. The beans were found to absorb the greatest amounts of water just before the time of full moon; the least about the time of new moon. The experiment was carried out in a specially designed laboratory. Weather conditions could have had no effect on the beans and it was concluded that the moon's influence was unconnected with temperature, light or humidity. These findings seem to confirm gardeners' observations of more than 3,000 years that the growing moon affects the bulk of seeds and plants and stimulates germination. Scientists are coming to suspect that changes in the earth's electromagnetic field may underlie the much remarked connection between the moon and plant growth. It is during the full moon that disturbances in the earth's magnetic field are said to be greatest.

At present all that can be said with certainty is that the cosmos seems clearly to influence the gardener's world. Yet traditional beliefs still stand in disarray, with contradictions and obscurities perplexing enough to daunt most ordinary gardeners. Perhaps further carefully controlled experiments may lift the mysteries from the realm of folk-myth and provide practical formulae for all to use. When this comes about, gardeners could at last have come to working terms with beliefs of great antiquity.

2

GROWING MAGIC

Gardeners of many periods have indulged a fancy for improving fruit
trees by white magic. Among the Elizabethans, for example, those de-
siring red or yellow apples bored a hole in the tree's trunk with an
auger, made water, mixed in pigment of the wished-for colour, poured
the liquid into the hole and stopped it with a pin of the tree's wood,
sealed with wax. A mulberry grafted on a white poplar produced
white mulberries; a peach on a red damask plum, much-coveted red
fruit. Scarlet apples ensued if (following the old principle of homoeo-
pathic magic) red roses grew by apple trees. A watering of urine was
also helpful: '*Pour faire pommes rouges, faut arouser larbre d'urine ou bien
planter des rosier pres des pommiers,*' wrote Andros in the manner of his
time. Many, no doubt, followed his advice. Elizabethan gardeners believed that grafting a sweet- onto a sharp-flavoured apple produced
fruit of dual tang (like the modern Cox's Orange Pippin) and that a
nutmeg or scented rose petal pushed into a graft gave fruit tinctured
with these scents.

Sweet-smelling flowers about the orchard encouraged, by pre-
cedent, sweet fruit: but the rank-odoured, such as elder, must be
banished. Acknowledging the same doctrine, fruit planters in North
Carolina still eat sugar as they work,[1] and Ozark gardeners maintain
that melons will be the sweeter if seed is steeped overnight in sweet
milk before planting. Old-time gardeners particularly valued stoneless
fruit and believed that if the 'marrow' were removed from a cherry
tree's branch, its fruit would form without stones. Such beliefs persist,

43

and as recently as fifty years ago, even in level-headed Maine, it was stoutly affirmed that apple twigs planted upside down would produce apples without cores. Since there are few records of disappointed gardeners who found these bizarre tricks wanting, a never-ending supply of sanguine experimenters, alive with hope, is to be inferred.

Could such fancies have a factual basis? As far as grafting is concerned it seems unlikely. Yet the Royal Horticultural Society's *Dictionary of Gardening* (1974) comments that even today old ideas survive: we are told, for example, of modern claims that pears have been made to grow on willows, although true grafting of such ill-assorted companions is improbable. Essentially scion and stock must have natural affinity, as varieties of the same species, as species of the same genus or as genera of the same family: the closer the relationship the more likely the graft is to take. Nevertheless, M. Daniel, at least, has claimed grafting achievements to delight an Elizabethan heart: for him sunflowers have grown on melons, chrysanthemums on tomatoes and asters on phlox. The old magic was not quite preposterous.

'MEERE IDLE TALES AND FANCIES'

Of a garden belief at least 400 years old, E. E. Street of Chichester wrote in *Notes and Queries*, 1903: 'I remember many years ago being shown some flowers at Midhurst which I was told were obtained by the planting of primroses upside down. In shape they were halfway between a primrose and a cowslip and were of maroon colour with a deep yellow eye.' The belief is light-heartedly extant today: the flower produced may be 'a glowing pink', 'merely darker' or 'variegated' and a cowpat on top of the planting assists the charm![2] Northamptonshire folk contended that a common yellow primrose fed with bullocks' blood would become deep red. In Ireland and Wales the primrose is a fairy plant in its own right and therefore particularly favoured for such charms. The Elizabethans laid red vermilion or cinnabar, blue azure or the yellow mineral orpiment at roots of lilies to modify the colour of the flowers; or steeped bulbs in red wine, just as Roman gardeners had soaked their lily bulbs in purple wine to induce purple tints. And, in recent years, following an old German tradition, gardeners in Illinois have advised shaking flowers when a rainbow spans the sky to cause them to develop by magic 'all the colours of the rainbow'.

Every gardener is familiar with the colour-changing propensities of the hydrangea—now pink, now iron-blue, now a muddy blend of the two—variations induced by chemicals in the soil. Devon gardeners call hydrangeas 'changeables'. In North Carolinan magic blue indigo was laid at hydrangea roots to cause a switch to blue flowers, and even sophisticated Victorian gardeners ground up *blue* slates and forked the dust about their hydrangea bushes. It is easy to claim success for such artifices: hydrangeas may bear blue flowers one year and pink the next in spontaneous changes of colour quite divorced from the gardener's actions. Other procedures turned wild flowers into garden varieties, or made flowers larger or double.

Scents too received attention. The Elizabethans steeped cloves in rosewater, bruised them and bound them about the roots of gilliflowers or carnations which they hoped would then bear prized clove-scented flowers, valued for cordials and 'sallets'.

Double flowers were controlled, said some, by the phases of the moon. Hugh Platt in *Garden of Eden* (1600) suggested: 'Make Tulippes double in this manner something by cutting them at every full moone before they bear, to make at length beare double.' Constant moving and transplanting was another solemnly performed device to induce doubleness—indeed, the concept may not be quite dead for a correspondent told me in 1974:

> My brother's wife came to tea one day and apologized for not bringing her sister with her, but she was busy taking her rhododendrons 'round the garden'. It seemed that she dug up the rhododendrons, put them on a wheelbarrow, wheeled them round the garden, returned them to their original site, dug the soil over and put them back in the same place. This was done every two years with outstanding results. This way, she said, one never lost a plant.[3]

Such remarkable beliefs had long credence but with the coming of scepticism (in all departments of life) and the growing isolation of human intellect from its unconscious roots and from magic, critics gathered. John Parkinson in *Paradisi in Sole Paradisus Terrestris* (1629) scorchingly dismissed gardeners' machinations as pointless:

... the rules and directions to cause flowers to be of contrary or different colours or sents [sic], from that they were or would be naturally, are meere fancies of men, without any ground or truth ... I have been as inquisitive as any man might be, of everyone I knew, that made any such report ... I have made tryall at many times, and in many sorts of plants, accordingly, and as I thought fit, by planting & transplanting them, but I could never see the effect desired, but rather in many of them the loss of my plants.

And in a final passionate broadside he derides

... rules and directions set down in bookes so confidently, as if the matters were without all doubt and question; whenas without all doubt and question I will assure you, that they are but meere idle tales & fancies, without all reason or truth, or shadow of reason or truth.

FIRST FRUITS

Lest a fruit tree that is bearing for the first time be discouraged, its fruit must be gathered with ceremony; in Normandy, to this day, first fruits are never picked at all but are left as a hostage to future performance. The first fruits of each season emblematize plenty to come. Harold Nicolson spoke in his *Diary* of the silent prayer he was always moved to murmur at the first cuckoo, the first asparagus and the first green peas of the season and found it strange that a man so rational and urbane as he could feel such stirrings.[4] In Michigan the first strawberry must never be eaten—'throw it where a bird will have it'—a genuflection to old gods.[5] When the first new potatoes of the Scottish season were dug it was important for each member of the family to have a taste—or the crop would rot: often roots were named for father, mother and children and the year's prosperity deduced from the potatoes to be counted on each.

'PUT A DEAD CAT UNDER THEM'

About 1450, Montezuma the Elder commenced the restoration of the fabled gardens of Huaxtepec in Mexico and sent to the tropical coast for vanillas, orchids and other rare plants and trees, and for gardeners to care for them. Planting ceremonies began: the gardeners fasted for eight days, drew blood from their ears, anointed the plants and offered dead quail to the god of flowers, after sprinkling the plants and soil with blood. They predicted that thus protected none would die, and indeed within three years every tree and plant was growing far more exuberantly than it had in its native soil. In ancient Greece and Crete bulls' blood was the appropriate libation to strengthen fruit-trees.

Less spectacularly, placation of plant gods by offerings of blood continues at least instinctively, masked today by knowing talk of the virtues of commercial dried blood and bonemeal. The phenomenon of animal sacrifices in the garden is obviously confused since, in point of fact, bones and flesh provide valuable plant nutrients: gardeners favouring sacrifice have plausible excuses for the indulgence of deep instincts. Many are convinced that fundamental substances ('a bit of the good stuff') must do more good than chemicals arriving in a sack and do not disguise their predilection for slaughterhouse products. On the theme of sacrifice, F. Taylor of Birmingham told the writer about an old gardener of his acquaintance, an expert rose-grower, who always said: 'Put a *dead cat* under them—then you'll get some roses!'[6] In Devon it is said (now humorously of course) that a smooth-fruited gooseberry bush planted over a dead cat will switch to hairy fruit in the following season.[7] It is hard to say where husbandry ends and sacrifice—in modern dress—begins.

Ted Humphris, head gardener at Aynho House, Northamptonshire, remembered in *Gardener's Glory* (1970) that about fifty years earlier when lifting a particularly fine violet plant he had found particles of bone, probably those of hen and rabbit, clinging to the roots. Mr Humphris drew the obvious conclusion; that a liberal dressing of phosphates in bone form had been applied to produce finer violets. He was to use this method himself in later years. But was it so simple? It is by no means certain that the depositor of the bones had anything so straightforward in mind: apparent commonsense may veil the true intention. In North Carolina today it is still believed that a 'sacrifice' of chicken skins near plants encourages growth;[8] in Northern Scotland a hundred years ago old gardeners declared that a mouse buried beneath an apple tree and a cat under a pear ensured heavy cropping. No word of phosphates there!

In Morocco a mouse, most prolific of breeders, is killed, laid at the foot of the tree, and doused with boiling water, to carry mouse blood and the attribute of abundance to the furthest roots. Like produces like and the tree will take this hint to step up its own breeding. In Kentucky, in another plain propitiation, an ailing pig is killed and buried under a barren apple tree which will then bear fruit. (The Romans had offered a pig when thinning a grove of trees with the words: 'Whether thou be god or goddess to whom this grove is dedicated, it is thy right to receive a sacrifice of a pig . . .') As explicit is the Yorkshire custom of burying tails of freshly docked spring lambs under every sapling poplar at planting time: 'I have tried this and found it made a big difference,' writes a Yorkshire gardener from Garton-on-the-Wolds.[9]

Here then are two of the numerous aspects of sacrifice: first, that a buried animal placates the plant spirit who is thus persuaded to permit fruiting; second, that by sacrificing a fecund animal its attributes are transferred to the plant or tree.

Not all sacrifices are fleshly. The valuable walnut, tree of Jove, brought to Britain by the Romans, has always enjoyed esteem among country people. When walnuts are felled in Suffolk it is common for a gold coin to be discovered among the roots. F. W. Baty writes from Gloucestershire: 'In this neighbourhood, when grubbing up old perry pear trees, a small piece of coal is found directly under the trees in so many cases as to make coincidence unlikely.'[10] And when in May 1877 ash tree stumps were taken up in the parish of Scotton, Lincolnshire, iron horseshoes were found under many of them by workmen who were quite familiar with the practice: 'It is to charm the tree,' they said gravely. The horseshoe is an ancient apotropaic device.

PLANTING TREES

The life of a tree, fruitful, flourishing or fading, is predestined at planting time. Mrs Edgar E. Randolph of Elon College, Alamance County, North Carolina, remembers that trees should never be planted with unwashed hands, a belief reminiscent of Robert Herrick's seventeenth-century firelighting charm:

> *Wash your hands, or else the fire,*
> *Will not teend to your desire.*

Hand-washing had earlier played a part in the Romans' ritual sacrifices to the gods at the planting of garlic, millet and lentils.

Wassailing in a Devon orchard firing at an apple tree. According to the *Illustrated London News* of 11 January 1851, . . . it is customary for the farmer to leave his warm fireside, accompanied by a band of rustics, with guns, blunderbusses, &c., presenting an appearance which at other times would be somewhat alarming. Thus armed, the band proceed to an adjoining orchard, where is selected one of the most fruitful and aged of the apple-trees. . . . The cider jug is then passed round, and, with many a hearty shout, the party fire off their guns, charged with powder only, amidst the branches, sometimes frightening the owl from its midnight haunt . . .

Above, a block used by Egenolph of Frankfort, publisher, about 1550, showing a gardener at work. *Below*, gardeners at Stonehill, Waddesdon, Buckinghamshire, England, about 1908; the young man in the foreground is wearing the traditional tape-tied baize apron, badge of the professional gardener.

Imitative magic plays a decisive role in tree-planting. If the planter warmly praises a prosperous friend as he works, the friend's affluence will attach itself to the tree. In Maryland a child does the planting, presenting the tree with his own energy and life expectancy: as with pruning, it is thought that if an old man does the work his waning sexual powers will quickly cause the tree to cease fruiting and die.

Germans believe that no tree unendowed with name and motto makes its mark. When Baron Bunsen visited Lepsius, the antiquary, in Berlin in 1857, he was asked to plant a commemorative tree, to which he gave this dedication:

> *Oak, I plant thee. Grow in beauty; straight and firm and vigorous stand!*
> Bunsen *is the name I give thee; flourish in the German land.*
> *From the house of Lepsius blooming, through the storms grow fair and free,*
> *And a shelter in the noonday to his children's children be!*[11]

Trees enjoy respect: in Morocco they are never uprooted without good reason lest they revenge themselves and cause a death in the gardener's family: misfortune readily afflicts the house of a tree destroyer. And should the tree's owner be struck accidentally by a branch he must never swear or complain, let alone break the branch in retaliation. On the contrary the *gardener* must apologize to the *tree* saying '*Ya benti chedjera, Semahi lia*'—'O Tree, daughter Tree, forgive me.'

LETTERS TO MICE

Some are still convinced that mice, rats, moles or groundhogs may be persuaded to leave a garden by polite invitation in the form of letters left in their burrows. A writer in an American gardening magazine spoke of this belief a few years ago and was ridiculed by the editor; but at once a hundred readers wrote vociferously endorsing the superstition. In 1888 the will of George Jessop of Kenilworth, Baltimore County, Maryland, was contested by relatives, arguing that Jessop, who had died aged eighty-four, was of unsound mind. A neighbour, Mr Howard, gave evidence that at the deceased's request in 1882 he had agreed to drive rats from his house by a letter asking them to go.

> They were to be sent past the stone house, and keep on up the hill, right
> past the church, and not go down the turnpike, or up the turnpike, and to

D

keep on until they came to the large white house on the right . . . it was
Captain Low's house and they would get plenty to eat there.

During the hearing the attorneys, their clients, the jury and court
officials and the public present were convulsed with laughter 'and
during the day the slightest allusion to the "rat story" was a signal for
a fresh outburst . . .'. Mr Jessop was of the opinion that many of the
rats had, indeed, moved on as requested.[12]

The idea is not new. Greek farmers cleared gardens of mice by
politely offering the creatures alternative accommodation, but promising retribution if the invitation were ignored. Before sunrise the well-
greased message was stuck upon an unhewn stone where the mice
could read it before eating it.

A popular American book on witchcraft published in 1972 advised
that unwanted creatures could be kept from a garden by a small straw
doll which included some material from the nuisance, such as fur or
feathers. No intruder would pass such a device buried on the garden
boundary.[13] In Florida three small loaves baked on Good Friday and
laid among bulbs keep mice away.[14]

Insects too could be controlled by magic. If the first butterfly of the
season could be caught before it could lay eggs, freedom for the year
from the depredations of the cabbage-white caterpillar was guaranteed.
One family party walking quietly to church in Devon in May 1825
was overtaken by a breathless fellow churchgoer, running at full speed,
hat and stick in hand. As he passed he exclaimed 'I shan't hat'en now!'
The first butterfly had eluded him. To shorten the life of one insect was
a symbolic blow at all its kind: in Northamptonshire wasps were similarly dealt with.

The Germans favoured another charm against caterpillars. After
sunset the housewife walked round her garden dragging a broom,
never looking behind her, murmuring conversationally: 'Good evening, mother caterpillar, you shall come with your husband to church,'
and if the garden gate were left ajar overnight, by morning every
caterpillar would have departed. Pests spoken to politely leave of their
own accord.

A folk-cure for jaundice widely followed in Britain and North
America until this century required that an uncorked bottle of the

patient's urine be thrown into a stream. As the urine mixed with the water so would the patient's skin lose its characteristic yellow tint. By similar magic, American gardeners dropped an *odd* number of Lincoln bugs and cutworms into a bottle and tossed it into running water; the pests would be washed away and simultaneously vanish from the garden.[15]

WASSAILING THE ORCHARD

Until the early twentieth century the custom of wassailing—from the Old English *wes hál*—'be in good health'—intended to encourage fruit trees to bear, was observed in many fruit-growing districts of England. It was an orchard rather than a garden custom, but there is also evidence of its practice on a quieter, more domestic scale. Its season ran from Christmas Day, 25 December, to Old Twelfth Day, 18 January, although Old Christmas Eve, 5 January, was perhaps the most usual day for the celebration, when the farmer and his men, carrying a jug of mulled cider, went into the winter orchard under dark skies and drank a cheerful toast by the best tree, in words such as:

> *Here's to thee, old apple tree!*
> *Whence thou may'st bud and whence thou may'st blow,*
> *And whence thou may'st have apples enow,*
> *Hats full, caps full,*
> *Bushel-bushel-sacks-full!*
> *And my pockets full too! Hurrah!*

The company bowed in salutation, rising heavily as though with sacks of fruit; cider was tossed over the roots and pieces of toast laid in the branches for the 'robin' (some said to Pomona, goddess of fruit-trees); and the party fired a salvo of rook-shot through the bare branches to awaken the tree-spirit to fresh endeavours. Robert Herrick, the Devon poet, explained expectations thus:

> *Wassail the trees, that they may beare*
> *You many a Plum and many a Peare;*
> *For more or less Fruits they will bring,*
> *As you doe give them Wassailing.*

As well as a welcome chance to prolong Christmas fun, an underlying sense of magic vital to apple husbandry accompanied the ceremony. A witness to Devon wassailing introduced it in recent years to the great apple-growing region of Yakima, Washington, but many feel that the superstitious unsophisticated form was the more attractive. A Horsted Keynes, Sussex, woman remembered that as a child early this century her grandfather had given her a penny to 'howl' or wassail his solitary garden apple-tree and to beat it with a stick; and in Surrey boys visited every tree in the garden, inserting the words 'mulberry', 'nut', 'fig' or 'currant' into their song, as required. The beehives were not forgotten.

Sharing among neighbours was a feature of Christmas, and the fruit-trees were not forgotten. In Germany and Switzerland, in a custom reminiscent of the offerings to walnuts in England, money was buried under the trees: in Montenegro, fragments of the charred Christmas log laid among the branches encouraged a good crop. Fruit-trees flattered by the receipt of gifts would be moved to bestow them.

The rules of fruit-tree husbandry are exacting. To fell a fruit-tree is ill-omened and approached with reluctance by many, as if to destroy the source of fruitfulness malimprints the life of the tree's owner. Trees must be thanked for fruit, lest they repay discourtesy with a poor crop. And libations are in order, in grafting as in wassailing. When in the 1920s the village grafter visited Arthur Savory's Worcestershire orchards each April he was traditionally 'paid by the piece' at a rate of 'three-halfpence a graft and cider', and while the quantity of cider was not specified it was vital to the bargain, for grafts 'unwetted' would not take. In Russia a peasant girl did the work—and at the very moment of grafting was 'herself subjected to treatment which was a clear imitation thereof'. With this plain hint, the graft was certain to grow!

The Elizabethans customarily left a branch uncut at pruning time 'to cherish the sap'—more accurately as an appeasement of the tree for such disrespectful interference. In recent years Miles Hadfield's Warwickshire gardener always 'half-pruned' his gooseberry bushes, following the axiom that you should 'leave half the bush for the birds'[16]—a practice admittedly with commonsense underpinning, for it does encourage birds to attack the buds of a part, rather than the whole, of the bush. But perhaps 'birds', like the 'robins' of wassailing, are in reality tree-spirits; the act perhaps conciliatory? The gooseberry, one of the 'lightning plants' described in chapter four, merits special respect.

'THEM'S FAMILY MATTERS . . .'

Within the doctrines of sympathetic magic, like creates like. An unfruitful tree can be stimulated by contact with human pregnancy or by emblematic 'crops' of weighty stones tied to its branches. Human and tree fertility are joined. In the Zürcher Oberland, Austria, and Bavaria, by magical analogy a cherry-tree will always bear abundantly if its first fruits are eaten by a woman who has just given birth to her first child. In Syria, a pregnant woman is persuaded to tie a rock to a fruit-tree's branches; in the process she transfers her fertility to the tree—but may suffer a miscarriage as a consequence. In an intricate charm of the Pacific Islands, two stones, one resembling a ripe and the other an unripe fruit, fertilize each breadfruit tree. The surrogate 'unripe fruit' is buried at the tree's foot, then, as the crop approaches maturity, it is replaced by the 'ripe fruit'. When the breadfruit have been safely harvested the stones are laid aside, their work done for that season. Yam-shaped or banana-shaped stones help their respective crops. The charm, in its variations, is universal; in Swabia and Sicily a barren tree stands bowed down by heavy stones all through spring and summer, to encourage autumn fruiting: such stones prevent a premature fall of fruit. Other shadowy arcana are suggested by the discovery by archaeologists in America of primitive stone axeheads deeply embedded in the heart-wood of trees, perhaps as tributes to nature spirits. Northern European peasants sometimes buried a stone axe at the field's edge in thanks for harvest.

The practice of hammering iron nails into fruit trees to induce bearing is fairly well known in both Britain and America although, as with many charms, its aspects are complex and much confused. One object —which presumes the tree's sentience—may be to bring a lazy tree to its senses; another to improve fruiting by beneficially inhibiting sap flow; a third to hinder witchcraft and the evil eye and their obviously adverse effects upon the crop. A palisade of nails in the orchard holds any witch at bay, for a witch's dread of iron, particularly in the shape of pins and nails which may 'prick' and 'blood' as well as halt her, is proverbial. The evasiveness of those who believe in 'nailing their trees' is surely significant, and is suggestive of a multi-function charm, with practical overtones probably of later introduction. Pragmatism alone would surely render such secretiveness quite unnecessary? There must also be magic and mystery. Whatever the true intention, the belief endures stolidly enough, particularly in out-of-the-way places: when Vance Randolph enquired about one nail-studded peach-tree in the Ozark Mountains he was given a typical reply when the tree's owner growled, 'Them's *family* matters,' and flatly declined to enlarge upon his reasons for using nails thus![17]

In another instance, among negroes of the southern United States, a 'hoodoo-man' or 'root doctor' drove five rusty nails into the heart of a cherry tree which had never blossomed and the following year the tree had to be supported under a record crop of fruit: a 'conjure' or charm (materials unspecified) was also wrapped in a rag and buried at the tree's foot. Since a hoodoo-man was invited to work the charm it seems clear that on this occasion at least the tree was felt to be under the encumbrance of a spell.

Of another charm, aimed, as the nailing may be, at controlling sap flow, William Brown of Stockleigh Pomeroy, Devon, whose family have been hedgers in the county for hundreds of years, writes: 'My father used to say, to make an apple or pear tree buck up and grow good fruit, you had to bore a hole in the tree's trunk and drive a green oak peg into it.' The specified use of *green oak* illuminates the antiquity of the belief, for the oak was sacred to Thor and Jupiter and venerated by the Druids as outstanding for all magical purposes. Any gardener using green oak in his orchard calls gods of thunderbolt and storm, high in the pantheons, to his aid.

Whipping and shooting recall idle trees to duty as fruitmakers and encourage the industrious to continue their efforts. As late as February 1930, after a poor year, trees at Huixtla, Mexico, were lashed severely, for there peasants believed that regular chastisement benefitted crops. Pennsylvanian German farmers whipped their peach trees on Good Friday, going straight from bed to orchard, speaking to no one on the way, for silence, concentrating the would-be sorcerer's thoughts upon his task, is an essential accompaniment to effective magic. In Thurgau, Mecklenburg, Oldenburg and the Tyrol, whipping took place during the Christmas season; in Sicily at Eastertide. The walnut tree, of stature and sacrifice, again merited special attention:

A woman, a whelp and a walnut tree
More you beat 'em, better they be!

Punishment of the indolent does not cease with beatings. In a pantomime to be seen in Moroccan orchards, the owner presents a minatory axe to a poor-yielding tree saying: 'If you won't give dates, I'm going to *kill* you'; and his servant answers humbly for the tree, 'Forgive me this time. Next year I will give plenty.' Phraseology and action show remarkable uniformity from one country to another. Dr Aston, British consul in Seoul during the nineteenth century, wrote that he had witnessed the same orchard ceremony in Japan, where it took place on the last day of the year. Villagers of Selangor, Malaya, assemble round a barren durian tree and a wizard strikes a feint blow at the delinquent with a hatchet to: 'Will you bear fruit or not? If you do not I shall fell you!' The contrite tree replies through a man stationed on a nearby mangosteen (the durian itself is unclimbable): 'Yes, I will now bear fruit. I beg you not to fell me.' Gashes are to be seen on most Moroccan fig-trees. The fig-tree genie is particularly spiteful and before a gardener may sit beneath his trees he must gash the bark to drive the elemental to a safe distance: and such a gash also intimidates the genie into allowing the tree to bear. Completing this array of international parallels are the Yorkshire recollections of Charlie Ross, aged 75, of Barmby Moor, who told the writer in 1974:

> When I was in my teens I was told of the owner of an apple orchard. One of his trees would not bear fruit so he went to it and said: 'I will *shoot* you if you don't bear apples this year.' But spring came and as usual there was no fruit. So he fetched his 12-bore shotgun and 'shot' the tree. The year after it was loaded with apples. I had a Balsam apple which had not fruited or flowered since I grafted it ten years before. Last year when it failed again I stood near it and said: 'Look, you useless tree, you have had nothing on you since I brought you to life, and I am now going to take my knife and cut your throat'—which I did with one long gash! This year it has quite a lot of apples.[18]

Apart from pure magic can there be benefits in such practices? Little in garden lore is devoid of all practicality, and behind the play-acting is sound commonsense. Whipping and shooting would undoubtedly knock off surplus fruit spurs and, by reducing the number a

tree must support, improve the crop. Bark damage could also be helpful in several ways, despite the risk of introducing disease with the
injuries.

In *Garden News*, 18 January 1974, G. Pailthorpe of Leicester wrote of
a remedy for aphis based on broken twigs, such as might well occur
during whipping. He had come upon the practice while holidaying in
a farming area of Switzerland and noticed that new growth on both
apple and pear trees had been partially broken and left hanging on the
branches to die. There seemed no obvious reason for this except to
cause the fruit, excellent in size and condition, to swell. Mr Pailthorpe
remembered that he had had difficulty in pruning his own trees back to
fruit buds: much new growth always reached high in late spring. So
the following year when the new shoots were about six inches long he
cracked them and left them hanging. He was amazed at the results.
Apples and pears were not only larger and unblemished but woolly
aphis was entirely absent. Mr Pailthorpe suggested that the smell of sap
from dying growth may repel aphis or perhaps that the insects cannot
breed on dying leaves. At the time of writing he had performed the
breaking for three years and, in a happy phrase, 'It has worked like a
charm every time.' Sap released in beatings, shootings and bark slittings
could well act as an insect deterrent. Low insect activity obviously
improves a crop.

Also sap-releasing was the Channel Islands practice of peeling back a
portion of the bark of an unfruitful peach-tree to allow a little 'humour'
to escape in 'bleeding the tree', phrases resembling those used by
medical practitioners of a procedure favoured until the nineteenth
century. And distinguished authorities confirm, from a non-super-
stitious viewpoint, the value of 'cutting a tree's throat'.

The eminent orchardist, Raymond Bush, observes that a tight con-
straining bark reduces sap flow and inhibits fruiting. Young trees with
soft bark often show long scars where the tree has sought relief itself
through natural splitting. Bush suggests that the remedy is to slit the
bark on the north, sunless side of the tree, in a single vertical cut. One
Peasgood Nonsuch apple which flowered well in a row of fruitful
neighbours never itself bore a good crop; he set his knife into the bark
and as the point went in, relieving internal pressure, the bark split
from crotch to root with an audible crack. The following year the tree

fruited excellently and continued to do so.[19] Another gardener, J. K. Murphy, of Roundup, Montana, wrote in *Organic Gardening*, July 1973, that a visitor looked at his non-bearing apple tree, murmured 'Bark bound!', whipped out his knife and gashed the bark. The tree at once began to bear. Slitting should be done between the pink bud and petal fall stages. The smallest slit or aperture in the bark makes possible natural spontaneous slitting: such damage is a likely result of whipping and wassailing.

The inevitable disturbance of the tree during these rituals would have other benefits. Organic gardeners know that insect pests may be dislodged from fruit trees by jarring: easily disturbed is the fruit-weevil, which then curls into a ball and drops to the ground. With this in mind, a nineteenth-century American gardener, Colonel T. Forest, of Germantown, Pa, ran a rope from the handle of his pump to a branch of his plum tree so that whenever a busy household drew water during the day the tree was 'gently agitated'. Liberty Hyde Bailey, a friend of William Kendrick, author of *The New American Orchardist* (1844), recommended a 'curculio (or weevil) catching cart', parked beneath the tree to receive falling pests, and favoured hitting trees with wooden mallets—although certainly not for magical reasons!

These explanations could of course be largely modern rationalizations: most gardeners are obviously a little shy of being caught working charms and would take care to have down-to-earth explanations to hand. Probably in their original and superstitious sense all these devices were aimed at stimulating the tree and keeping the tree-spirit under suitable control. The striking ubiquity of word and action in orchard rites—to be found from Malaya to Japan, from North Carolina to Montana, Bulgaria to Sicily, Morocco, Suffolk and Yorkshire—is quite impossible to miss. It could be argued that the superstitions spread with travellers from one country to another, but this seems unlikely. The distances are immense, the practices firmly established before the ease of modern communications: this explanation may therefore be dismissed. In fact the customs, expressing man's innate relationship with his fruit-trees, must have sprung up spontaneously in widely differing cultures. Like superstitions surrounding stones and metals, their ideas lie near to the heart of magic.

BURNING THE WITCH

Gardeners enjoying the last flicker of emotions which underlay the old fire festivals of Europe confess to exultation as the flames from bonfires leap crackling into autumn skies. Christmas, Lent, Easter, Beltane and Midsummer fires, common as recently as one hundred years ago, not only magically quickened the sun's strength and plant growth with their genial warmth but destroyed baleful influences, saving fields from blight and houses from storms—disasters attributed to witchcraft.

Fires sparkled in the cold air of Christmas and Twelfth Night, about the time of the old solstitial festival; and as the flames danced upwards villagers in Normandy leapt round the fires dashing blazing torches against tree trunks, scattering charred twigs and ashes far to fructify their gardens. Children, barred from more dangerous activities, lighted hay wisps against the trees, a charm to rid orchards of moss, moles, caterpillars and field mice. The longer the ceremony the better the harvest.

Lenten fires came next. Until about 1840, in the province of Hainaut, Belgium, on the first Sunday of Lent—'Little Scouvion'—children ran through orchards shouting

> *Bear apples and bear pears*
> *And cherries all black*
> *To Scouvion!*

and hurling flaming brands through the trees' branches. For good measure the ritual was repeated on the following Sunday—'Great Scouvion'. Charred sticks from Easter Saturday's 'Burning of Judas' (earlier the pagan fire burning 'Winter') were buried in the garden to save the crops from hail; and the ashes of oak, beech and walnut, charred in the sacred Easter needfire, mixed with seed to be sown in spring, promoted fertility. Gardens so treated enjoyed miraculous exemption from all evils. So far as the light of the Easter fires shone into the garden, so far would the crops prosper.

The great summer-welcoming fires, man's response to the powers of darkness abroad on May Day, followed. 'Fire! Blaze and burn the witches!' shouted the dancers. Midsummer fires saluted the pre-eminent sun and in the apple counties of Somerset and Herefordshire 'blessed the apples'. Gardeners of Roscommon, Ireland, still sprinkle midsummer ashes on their plots for luck. These fires, so frequent as to be almost regular fumigation, were practical as well as magical. Up to the early twentieth century on Vermont farms sulphur was burned in the cracks of the bark of fruit trees while they were in blossom, to kill insects likely to damage the crop: children were given the task of scraping dead bark off old trees and exposing the insects' hiding-places. At the writer's home in Surrey, along the garden fence bordering the railway line stood twelve apple trees, which until March 1928 were enveloped twice hourly throughout the day by a cloud of smoke from passing steam trains. Then the line was electrified, smoke ceased to blow, and immediately the trees became infested with pests and remained so. Insects intensely dislike smoke and ash and who can say with certainty that the fire festivals were entirely preoccupied with magic? Was their target not as much the caterpillar as the witch?

SEX AND PLANTS

In the primitive world, plant and human reproduction seemed ineluctably linked and such ideas survived later than is generally realized. Vance Randolph wrote that in the spring of 1920 in south-west Missouri a fisherman from Joplin walking through the woods at dawn saw a man and woman, both stark naked, chasing each other up and down a small field. Randolph, acquainted with these people, quiet, hardworking, church-going, backwoods folk, mentioned the story to a neighbour, long resident in the district, who said that he had himself heard of such rituals which were supposed to make the corn grow tall. They had doubtless been introduced by settlers from Tennessee, Kentucky or Virginia, but no one, to his knowledge, believed in them now.

Later Randolph got to know hundreds of elderly people in the Ozarks and found that settlers had indeed believed that newly cleared fields benefitted from nude skylarking. Sowers of seed must work naked. Although in the 1950s Randolph admitted that the rituals were no longer widely practised (indeed some claimed never to have heard of them) he knew of isolated areas where they had been carried out less than thirty years before.

Tales were told of one family in south-west Missouri whose land produced turnips of almost magical size. Before sunrise on 25 July four grown-up daughters and one son, all stripped naked, did the planting. The boy began work in the middle of the plot and the girls skipped round him as he sowed, shouting, 'Pecker deep! Pecker deep!' When sowing was completed the whole party rolled together in the dust. One elderly neighbour said that, although there seemed no sense to it, the family did, undoubtedly, grow the finest turnips on the creek.

In McDonald County, Randolph was shown a clearing in a hollow where a man and two naked women romped and tumbled in a newly prepared garden plot. His informant said nothing of crops, only that the trio were members of the New Ground Church and that the ritual was part of their religion. Whatever the explanation Randolph later saw turnips growing there too. Another informant, an old man in Aurora, Missouri, spoke of the settlers sowing flax just before sunrise. The woman walked ahead; behind came the man throwing seed against her thighs; both recited a rhyme with the words 'Up to my ass, an' higher too!' When the work was done they lay down and 'had a good time'. No outsider, said Randolph's informant, must witness the ritual or hear the song or the crop would fail.

Yet another farmer near the Missouri–Oklahoma border told of the practice among 'peckerwood' folk who lived there in the 1890s. When their sweetcorn was planted the owner of the garden took his wife to the corn patch at midnight and made her strip and run round the crop three times. He then threw her to the ground and 'have at it till she squealed like a pig'. This, it was claimed, saved the corn from a battery of evils—frost, drought, cutworms and crows.[20]

In Europe (whence the American custom must have come) rolling and leaping high homoeopathically encouraged crops to grow, and a frieze in the Roman city of Pompeii shows the religious act of copulation performed to stimulate crops and rain. In similar vein many old gardeners in the United States are convinced that good cucumbers will only result from seed sown before daylight on 1 May by a well-endowed man, naked and in the prime of life. The size of the cucumbers depends upon the visible virility of the sower. Cucumbers sown by women, children or old men never amount to much. It is the plainest magic.[21]

Similar beliefs are found in many parts of the world. When the rice is blooming in Java, the husbandman and his wife visit the fields at night to make love among the plants, which take the hint and set the maximum amount of seed. In the Pacific Islands a few couples are appointed to have intercourse precisely as the first seeds are dropped into the ground, thus transferring their own sexual energy to the plants.[22] In Illinois and Louisiana it is said that any crop—even the merest token—planted by a pregnant woman will do well.

Another set of traditional beliefs and practices hints at half-forgotten fertility rites to ensure the germination of seed. Within living memory East Anglian farmers have been known to take off their trousers and to sit down on the bare soil of the seedbed to test the earth's warmth and suitability for sowing. (Yorkshire gardeners like to sow when the land is 'on heat'—steaming moistly in the hot spring sunshine. Seed sown then will be up in a day or two. The phrase is felicitous.) Among the North American Indians the women did the seed sowing while the men were away hunting and making war. When the planting season arrived the women would waylay a young man of their tribe as he returned from these adventures, strip him of his buckskin trousers and sit him on the bare earth of the garden. If he shivered it was still too cold to plant! Since a hand or foot laid on the earth would have been just as good an indicator of its warmth it is tempting to see the contact between the genitals (in the case of the Indians of a *young* man) and the soil as expressive of a fertility procedure.

Farmers in the Algarve of Portugal will never allow their virgin daughters to climb up into almond or olive trees in bloom, lest through sympathetic magic the girls' virginity makes the trees barren. People aid plants and plants can aid people. Among the Kara-Kirghiz barren women rolled on the ground beneath apple trees in the hope of conceiving. Apples have long been fertility symbols: even in stolid England a good apple year was once reckoned a promising one for twins. But otherwise there is disappointingly little in the English tradition to match the more dramatic fertility rituals of other countries. (As recently as 1972 an American woman gardener was advised by a friend to burn one of her undergarments on a small bonfire in the corner of her garden and to sprinkle the ashes on the seedbed when she had finished spring planting. This would make the plants grow. The specification of an *undergarment* clearly suggests a sexual rite.) Growers of prize chrysanthemums in Staffordshire are said to believe in watering their plants with the urine of a pregnant woman, but it is not clear whether this is magic or common sense. The daily nitrogen excretion in urine is given as in the range of 10.26–20.34 grams, approximately 84 per cent of this in the form of urea. There seems to be no information, however, that the composition of urine changes significantly during pregnancy (except, of course, for the hormonal composition, which varies strikingly). In this case commonsense would seem to win. But, as always, absence of evidence of magical practices of this kind is by no means evidence of their absence: the quintessence of powerful magic is always silence, discretion and lack of witnesses.

Modern research has clothed the emotional aspects of the superstitions. Pierre Paul Sauvin of West Patterson, New Jersey, an electronics specialist and investigator of ESP and remote hypnotism, believes that plants react to human emotions. When on holiday with a girl friend eighty miles from his plants he found that when the couple made love the plants reacted with high peaks on a tone oscillator to which they were linked: as orgasm occurred the pointer went to the limit of the dial. Dr Marcel Vogel, an American researcher in plant sensitivity, has noticed that when his laboratory plants are attached to lie detectors, no reaction is recorded until the lab group's talk turns to sex; then all the plants respond to the heightened emotions of people considering eternal verities! Further research will no doubt have something to add: it seems that the ancients could well have been right.

SEEDS AND CUTTINGS

Magically, vegetable growth is stimulated by comparisons with the human body—indicating clearly the gardener's visual expectations. Sowers in Illinois recite as they scatter cabbage seed:

> *As round as my head*
> *And as big as my butt!*

and for turnips:

> *As round as my head and as big as my thigh,*
> *And some for the* neighbour *who lives close by*

—surely an echo of propitiation? Prudent gardeners visit their parsnips daily with later reminders:

> As long as my arm
> As thick as my wrist

—and shake the tops of the plants to drive the point home![23]

Deviations from the norm at all times intimate disaster: to miss a row at sowing portends a death within the twelvemonth in the gardener's family: in Ireland, to omit a row at potato setting imperils the whole crop.[24] Myra Jensen of Morrison, Iowa, describes as particularly ominous the portent if the gardener does not notice his mistake until plants appear: she calls this superstition Danish but in fact it is universal. A traveller in mid-Cardiganshire about 1850 noticed an incongruous row of turnips in the midst of a Nonconformist minister's potato patch. When the growing potatoes revealed their secret the fearful owner had at once seized and scattered a handful of the nearest seed to thwart malignant fate.

In the Ozarks peppers do best if the planter is in a temper—peppers are *hot*!; even better if planting is done by a lunatic! Negroes of the American South make children plant vegetable seeds so that seeds and children grow together. Estonian peasants wrap a small stone tightly in a white linen rag and bury it in the garden to encourage firm, white cabbage heads for sauerkraut; and since prickly leaves are undesirable in artichokes they snap off the sharp end of the seed at planting time to magically blunt the leaves. A shadow of the ancient reverence due to a religious rite clings to seed-sowing: if the sower laughs as he sets his sweetcorn the grains will be irregularly spaced on the cob and the whole crop indifferent.

In another application of imitative magic, if corn cobs, bean pods or potato peelings are burned after the vegetables have been prepared for table, hot sun will similarly scorch the growing crop: Ozark farmers take particular care to throw vegetable remains into *running* water— to ensure adequate rainfall for the rest of the season, or bury them in a corner of the garden, returning an oblation of vegetables to the soil whence they came. Whole and parts remain one, even after harvest: to destroy one without due precautions is to jeopardize the crop.

To coastal dwellers tides are visible, daily signs of increase; a rising tide is analogous to swelling vegetables, and Alabama negroes plant watermelons at a floodtide for largest yields. In Nova Scotia potatoes planted as the tide rises and late at night start to grow with the new day.

Another significant survivor among beliefs is that the gardener should spit into the seed drill after completing sowing. F. A. Welti of Blechingley, Surrey, writes: 'I don't know if this is some sort of offering to the gods, but it certainly seems to keep small rodents from the more succulent seeds.' Saliva, like urine, is a secretion close to man's essential nature and a frequent ingredient of charms. Conciliation of the Earth Mother may indeed be the purpose, but spitting is also a powerful weapon against the evil eye and even today is in daily use for this purpose in Greece and other Mediterranean countries. In the garden context it could be another protective device, like the sign of the cross.[25]

Some gardeners will never plant when a north wind is blowing, for the old superstition that aphides (irrespective of their normal reproduction which is complex) are actually *brought* by the wind dies hard: wind rather than insects often receives the name 'blight'.

> *For oft engendered by the hazy north,*
> *Myriads on myriads, insect armies warp,*
> *Keen in the poisoned breeze; and wasteful eat,*
> *Through buds and bark, into the blackened core*
> *Their eager way.*

Thus James Thomson, graphically. The misapprehension seems understandable enough, for when the north wind blows aphides appear overnight. Sheltered trees are unaffected and a single screened branch may escape although the rest are encrusted with insects. Aphides apparently lack wings yet cluster on the highest branches exposed to soughing wind. It follows that wind must have brought them![26]

Many gardeners refuse to give thanks for cuttings or seeds lest they do not grow: to imply a *fait accompli*, to hint at premature success, however lightly, is dangerous. Rosemary has special rules: 'It must not be bought, nor must a piece be stolen. It must be given by a sincere friend with a gracious speech such as "I give you this rosemary gladly and I hope that it will grow with you".' Louisiana gardeners say 'When you give a cutting or plant "with a good heart" it will grow.'[27] 'The more you gives 'em away, the better they grows,' is the saying:

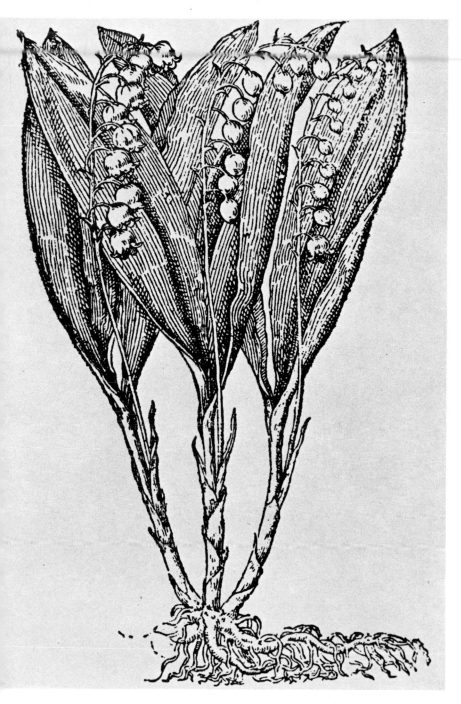

Lily-of-the-valley grows best by 'her husband', Solomon's seal.

Griggling in the orchard. Although it is in theory for the birds or fairies that small apples are left on the trees after the main picking, in practice a blind eye is turned while the children make away with as much as they can.

An old aunt of mine, the late Mrs Stanbury of Furze Park, Launceston, Cornwall, was a wonderful gardener all her life. She was well over 80 when she died last year. Her belief was always that the more you give of your plants through roots and cuttings, the more they will increase and grow. This certainly seemed to be true in her case: she had such a wide variety of plants and shrubs that many gardeners came to her for advice and she gave away hundreds of plants in her time.[28]

And:

A friend, a Croat lady now resident in Stoke-on-Trent, tells me that there is a widespread half-humorous belief there (although Stoke gardeners are no less generous than those elsewhere) that if it is to prosper the cutting or plant must be *stolen*. It is thus not unusual for one gardener to say to another, 'Yes, of course, come and steal a piece some time!' The fellow-gardener will then choose a time to creep furtively upon the neighbour's garden and 'steal' the coveted plant with no moral obloquy. It is felt that such a booty will grow better than any plant handed over publicly and politely. One of my friend's informants was an amused policeman who himself has done a certain amount of non-sinful stealing and being stolen from.[29]

Cuttings from a neglected, disused garden, purveying destructive magic, must be shunned or they will 'poison' the receiver's garden. Unused cuttings are never burned or those which have rooted will sympathetically shrivel; and, for success, cuttings should always be struck in threes—apparently in recollection of the Holy Trinity,[30] but in fact the belief is far older: in pagan antiquity three was a magical number of great potence and many old charms required that actions or words be performed or spoken thrice.

E

3

SEASONS AND SAINTS' DAYS: THE ROLLING YEAR

For many centuries, until the introduction of almanacs, the gardener's year was paced by sun, seasons, the rising and setting of stars, saints' days, sprouting leaves and migrant birds. Many reminders are still in use, and we recall the wisdom of sowing parsley on Good Friday, of planting when cuckoo and swallow arrive and of setting shallots at the winter solstice. The pious prune their roses on St Patrick's Day; the worldly with Grand National Day as a guide.

THE GATE OF THE YEAR

Modern almanacs arrange the seasons illogically: in northern hemispheres spring and autumn begin, astronomically speaking, at the equinoxes, and winter and summer at the solstices: spring opens about 21 March, summer about 21 June, autumn about 21 September and winter about 21 December. The winter solstice marks the true beginning of the gardener's year—sap is down, days dark, air cold, but yet on this magical shortest day the sun reaches its southernmost point in the ecliptic and begins to climb through winter skies to turn the seasons to green leaves and summer. This happy pagan moment was tethered by the tactful early Church to the feastday of St Thomas the Apostle, 21 December:

> *St Thomas Gray, St Thomas Gray*
> *Longest night and shortest day.*

The mild perennial called 'St Thomas's onion' is traditionally planted at midwinter and harvested at the summer solstice—analogous magic to cause the crop to increase to maximum size in step with lengthening days. The name 'St Thomas's onion' imprecisely applies to many onions: among them the Potato Onion, *Allium Cepa*, the Egyptian Onion, *Allium Cepa aggregatum*, and the Welsh onion, *Allium fistulosum*, all of which, propagated by offsets, not seed, crop three months before other varieties and, as a bonus, are not attacked by onion-fly.

The mantle of solstitial onion lore has now largely fallen upon the shallot, *Allium ascolonicum*: the RHS *Dictionary* advises that the old instruction to plant on the shortest day and to harvest on the longest should be heeded, in spirit at least. Many agree. One correspondent, adding a Christian variant, writes: 'The old man who sells me my shallots tells me that the best day—traditional Cheshire lore—to plant shallots is *Christmas Day*.'[1] Such notions attach to certain other vegetables also: 'My mother, whose parents farmed on the Newdigate estate near Nuneaton, said of broad beans: "Plant on the shortest day to gather on the longest."'[2] "'Tis time the broad beans were in! I know some who sets 'em on the shortest day—and they nivver seems to hurt,' declares a Buckinghamshire gardener.

CHRISTMASTIDE

The calendar changes of 1752 (see appendix) at first confused gardeners in both England and her North American colonies. Christmas Day 'New Style' was 24 December; 'Old Style', 6 January: Christmas beliefs tended to be applied indiscriminately to either style. If, for example, the sun shone through the apple boughs on Christmas Day (Old or New) a fine 'blowth' or blossoming could be expected; if the day were cloudy the trees might die. In North Carolina beans and cabbages are still planted between the New and Old Christmas for maximum yields. The season's sanctity benefits the crop. It is perhaps worth remembering that as late as the thirteenth century the year began on Christmas Day (formerly the midwinter birthday of the sun god), which served to heighten the stature of the day. Many beliefs of pagan origin, concerned with 'new beginnings', seed-sowing included, continue transmuted by Christianity and now linked with Christ's birthday.

Christmas weather is portentous. An east wind on Old Christmas

Day, 6 January, promises baskets of fruit: '*Année venteuse, Année pommeuse,*'—'a windy year, good for apples,'—say the French; and 'Frost year, Fruit year.' Nova Scotia farmers still speak of snow as 'the poor man's fertilizer' and of a 'million dollar snowfall'; the Russians believe that 'crops are as comfortable under snow as an old man under his fur cloak'; and four hundred years ago in England, Francis Bacon, repeating a belief old in his time, wrote: 'Snow cherisheth the ground and anything sowed in it.'

Why should wild rough weather be esteemed, contradicting the more facile view that mild airs please gardeners? Frost (called 'God's plough' in Worcestershire) breaks up the ground and fines the tilth: low temperatures destroy insect pests. (After the severe winter in England of 1962–3, for example, delphinium losses were unusually low because slugs did not survive to make their usual attack: in 1975, following a frost-free winter, aphides made disastrous inroads.) Frost-hard ground retains soil nutrients otherwise washed away by winter rains: pests fall from winter-buffeted fruit trees. Today apple trees are kept low to allow easy pruning but old gardens show venerable hoary veterans, with confused branches so difficult to trim that, human nature being what it is, the work was probably neglected. To such trees, winter gales, eliminating weak and dead branches and superfluous fruit buds, would do nothing but good.

That the weather of the year's first quarter determines the harvest, not the rain and sun experienced by growing crops, is a European belief of ancient origin. Dr Herbert Hanus of the Institute of Horticulture and Plant Cultivation, Weihenstephan, West Germany, supports this view and using weather records and equations has been able accurately to forecast harvests three or four months earlier than is possible by conventional methods. According to German reports in April 1967 Dr Hanus's forecast was for a yield of 78cwt a hectare, when the conventional estimate was 69·2cwt and the actual yield 83·4cwt. The 1971 prognosis was poor because of drought, but Hanus predicted a record harvest, which duly came about. Processes in atmosphere and soil in winter have decisive effects on growth: nitrogen, for example, may be leached from the soil by excessive rain or converted into forms most beneficial to plants. Findings seem to vindicate the peasant beliefs of centuries.[3]

ST BRIDE, CANDLEMAS AND ST VALENTINE

The first day of Celtic Spring, 1 February, was Christianized as the day of St Bride, the White Goddess of England, Scotland and Ireland, whose symbols were the spring lamb and the dandelion. On St Bride's Day, outdoor work begins in Ireland. The saint promised that after *her* day every *second* day would be hard and dry and St Patrick that after *his* day—17 March—*every* day would be dry.[4]

All over North America, 2 February, Candlemas, is Groundhog Day, an occasion noted in every newspaper. If the groundhog emerges from his burrow then and sees his own shadow, frost and snow are still to come, but a cloudy day means happily that winter is nearly done. Similarly in seventeenth-century England:

> . . . 'tis an omen bad, the yeomen say,
> If Phoebus shows his face the second day.

Groundhog Day is particularly ceremonious at Punxsutawney, Pennsylvania, 'Groundhog Capital of the World'. German settlers there believed that *any* animal emerging from his burrow on 2 February and seeing his own shadow would quickly retire again in anticipation of a further six weeks of 'second winter'. The belief became attached specifically to the groundhog. In 1886 the editor of the local newspaper, the *Punxsutawney Spirit,* named a group which sought out and honoured the groundhog the 'Punxsutawney Groundhog Club' and today it has members and chapters across America. The original groundhog weather station was on Gobblers Knob, a hill overlooking the town. Only its principal resident groundhog Phil ('Seer of Gobblers Knob') could properly interpret a shadow on 2 February. The first official shadow forecasting took place in 1887. Every year the Weather Scouts, Inner Circle and Faithful Followers trek to Gobblers Knob in the early morning of 2 February to visit the 'hallowed burrow' and to interview the Seer, record the shadow and announce the forecast to the world. The 'Great Prognosticator' has yet to make a mistake.

Many gardeners in Missouri and Arkansas, homes of tradition, remembering the Old Style calendar, celebrate Groundhog Day on 14 February, Candlemas Old Style, now St Valentine's Day. In 1933 when 2 February dawned clear and 14 February lowering, Vance

Randolph in Greene County, Missouri, saw with amusement, 'fur-riners' prepare for six weeks' more winter, while the old-timers, secure in their knowledge, cast aside their sheepskin coats and began to dig their gardens. Inevitably some garden beliefs have switched from Old to New Style, partly because St Valentine's Day, nearly two weeks later, is kindlier to planting. Styles now blend and adjurations march equably together:

> At Candlemas Day,
> 'Tis time to sow beans in the clay

wrote William Ellis in *The Modern Husbandman* (1750): in 1974 Cecil Atkins confirmed the saying as still well known round Waddesdon, Buckinghamshire, only a few miles from Ellis's farm; other gardeners may apply the same instructions to St Valentine's Day. Onion sowing is properly done on St Valentine's Day in North Carolina; English gardeners, on the other hand, are advised to sow *after* St Valentine's, 'when cats are on the prowl', suggesting warm spring nights of 'grow-ing'—and mating—weather.[5] It is a day specially fortunate for planting garden peas, lettuces, sweet peas and cabbages: one year when 14 February happened to fall upon a Sunday (a forbidden day for garden work) the residents of Kingston, Arkansas, anxious to comply strictly with the rules, rose before dawn to plant their lettuces, so as not to be caught violating the Sabbath by their neighbours!

Arthur Randell, a lifelong Norfolk Fenman, tells us that his father always walked into the garden early on 14 February to see if the trees were 'on the drip', which promised a good year for peas and beans. If the morning were dry he shook his head gloomily and pronounced that they would be 'ate up by lice'.[6] But in Dorset the self-same pro-cedure applied to Candlemas: '*N'importe*,' wrote one, 'the weather prophet coolly moves on his peg and goes on predicting with equal confidence!'

LEAP YEAR BEANS

In a 'leap year', every fourth year, February has 29 days—as we all know. Proper order is overturned in the 'ladies' year': girls propose to men and beans grow backwards in their pods. 'The eye is to the point, in other years to the strig [stalk],' a Surrey labourer solemnly assured

Squire Leveson-Gower of Titsey in 1888, a leap year. The squire investigated and wrote astringently: 'I have opened several pods of this year's growth and find the eye is to the point—and it probably will be so next year!' But a correspondent in the *Grantham Journal* of 22 September unreservedly agreed: 'It has been discovered that all kinds of Windsor and French beans this year have been produced in the pods in the reverse position to that which is usual.' Investigators might like to remember that 1980 is a leap year.

SAINTS DAVID, CHAD AND PATRICK

The days between the feasts of Saints David and Chad (1 and 2 March) and that of Benedict (21 March) are for pea- and bean-sowing:

> *Sow beans or peas on David and Chad,*
> *Be the weather good or bad;*
> *Then comes Benedict,*
> *If you ain't sown your beans—*
> *Keep 'em in the rick.*

When sweetpea growing became popular in the eighteenth century the belief expanded to embrace the flowers too. Sweetpeas sown on St Patrick's Day have larger more fragrant flowers if the work is done before sunrise. The day is deemed good in Buckinghamshire for onion-sowing, writes Cecil Atkins, but perhaps most generally observed was St Gregory the Great's Day, 12 March, so notable a date for this purpose that Lancashire cottagers dubbed it 'Gregory-gret-Onion'. In Wales the first daffodil of the year is said to bloom on St David's Day to honour the saint.

On his day, 17 March, St Patrick 'turns the warm side of the stone uppermost' and the first potato planting is done in Ireland: a dilatory gardener who misses this signal date may remedy his omission by saying 'praise be to St Patrick' as he drops each potato into its hole. Mrs O'Regan writes from County Cork that her father always made a point of pruning his rambler roses on St Patrick's Day, following a custom common in southern Ireland.[7] Thanks to immigrants the reputation of St Patrick's Day is as lustrous in the United States as it is in Ireland, for planting peas and 'Irish potatoes' (as opposed to sweet potatoes) and for transplanting from cold frames under the saint's beneficent eye. Maryland gardeners believe the day proper for cabbage planting but—in a pagan elaboration—the work must be done before dawn by a gardener wearing his night clothes: cabbages thus started are certain to 'head up well'.[8]

SPRING WEATHER

Late snow is beneficial. A fall after the onions are set is 'onion snow' and Cecil Atkins reports from Waddesdon: 'We always get a bit of "daffodil snow" after the daffodils have come into flower!' Warm days at the end of March or at the beginning of April bring the blackthorn into blossom (blackthorn usually blooms from 23 March in southern Ireland, 30 March in south-west England, 9 April in the English Midlands and 26 April in eastern Scotland) and 'blackthorn winter' follows, damaging young plants with chill winds and low temperatures: in the nineteenth century this cold weather was attributed by Professor Erman of Berlin to the showers of meteors, or 'shooting stars' (Lyrids, 20–22 April, and Aquarids, 2–6 May), through which the earth passes at about this time with a consequent lowering of temperatures. But the term may apply equally to the days of the 'ice-saints'; Mamertus, 11 May, Pancras, 12 May, Servatius, 13 May, Boniface, 14 May: in a late year the blackthorn is still blooming then and the French say, 'The days of the ice-saints do not pass without frost.' In the southern United States a similar reputation clings to 'dogwood winter', a boreal spell always to be expected when the dogwood—which has absorbed much of the European lore of blackthorn and mulberry—is in blossom.[9] In England old-timers among gardeners see menace in the sight of yellow brimstone butterflies among spring flowers: 'A bad sign; they yaller butterflies among the daffies brings hard weather.'

But, whatever the weather, it is the time for potato 'chitting'. K. H. Walpole of Heacham records a unique Norfolk belief: 'A neighbour on the allotments at Thornham, told me in the 1960s that when he puts a tray of seed potatoes in a bedroom to sprout he also places in the room a bowl of water so that any frost would go to the water, and not to the potatoes!'[10]

BLIND DAYS AND PLANTING SIGNS

In England the first three days of April—'blind days'—are ill-omened for seed sowing: in the United States the like reputation attaches to the first days of May, recalling the witches' revelry at Beltane, May Eve, or, in Germany, Walpurgis Night. Any Ozark gardener who dares to plant on the first three days of May is regarded as a heedless fool, however inviting the weather!

Everywhere gardeners look to budding leaves as planting guides. Of a typical rhyme:

> *Plant kidney beans if you be so willing,*
> *When elm leaves are as big as a shilling.*
> *When elm leaves are as big as a penny,*
> *You must plant beans if you mean to have any,*

one correspondent writes: 'It was handed down from my father and grandfather: I always plant my kidney beans to this old saying.'[11] Some specify the required leaf size as that of a farthing (a now obsolete small copper coin about the size of a cent) but the principle is much the same. The standard is visual and clearly recognizable by all.

Iowa gardeners watch for sprouting oak-leaves; and American Indians for elm, hickory and whiteoak in the hills, osage orange or *bois d'arc* (related, significantly, to the mulberry) in the plains, waiting for leaves the size of squirrels' ears. In Kentucky and North Carolina apple blossom time favours pea-planting: the Danes set their onions as the cherry blooms.[12] And at least one Cornish gardener looks for a growing moon, earth 'white and dry', and both thorn and gooseberry in leaf before committing his runner beans to the soil.[13]

Frost governs the gardener's spring programme:

> *When the dogwood flowers appear*
> *Frost will not again be here,*[14]

an American axiom, is matched in England by similar sayings about mulberry leaves which are never seen until frost is safely over for the year. The mulberry, a tree acutely sensitive, is last to show green buds in spring and first to lose its leaves at the merest hint of autumnal frost. On 6 April 1865 a parishioner drew the attention of a Huntingdon-shire clergyman to the 'wise-tree'—the mulberry—'which hadn't put out a mossel o' show . . . it isn't silly like some trees as puts out their leaves early and then gets nipped . . . you may rest content on the wise-tree telling you when you may be safe against frosses.' This valuable sign, equally familiar to Rome, is mentioned by Pliny.

The husbandmen of ancient Greece and Rome valued as planting signs the cluster of stars called The Pleiades, Hen and Chickens or Seven Sisters; in South Africa the 'hoeing-stars'. Winter sowings were undertaken only when these stars vanished from sombre autumn skies, early in November. *Multi ante occasum Maiae coepere; sed illos exspectata seges vanis elusit aristis* (Many have begun to sow before Maia's setting, but the looked-for crop has mocked them with an empty yield) wrote Virgil in his *First Georgic*. Maia, one star of The Pleiades, often stands for them all.

Boötes, with Arcturus, was another guide:

> Yet, if you choose to sow the vetch or homely kidney-bean and scorn not the care of the Egyptian lentil, setting Boötes will send you no doubtful signs. Begin, and carry on your sowing to midwinter's frosts.

The arrival of migrant birds signifies imminent summer warmth. Ozark farmers await the arrival of martins from the south (after which there will be no more frost) and the first cooing doves of spring, then plant immediately. American Indians listen for the whippoorwill calling his Indian name of *Wekolis* to remind them of planting. The appearance of the turkey-buzzard or American vulture is for them another sign. In southern Scotland peas are never set until there is sight and song of the swallow, harbinger of summer. Cheshire gardeners still look out for the yellow wagtail: when on 11 April 1938 a yellow wagtail flew across the fields of one farm and settled, appropriately enough, in some potato drills, a farmer said that this reliable sign that planting might begin had been familiar to him all his life; the wagtail was called the 'potato-dropper' or 'potato-setter'. If the cuckoo-bird, let out of her basket by the Old Woman at Heathfield Fair on 14 April 'to start lawful spring in England', arrives earlier, frost will blight the apple blossom, say Sussex gardeners. In Devon and Dorset the first fluting wood-notes of the cuckoo are linked with potatoes:

> *When you hear the cuckoo shout,*
> *'Tis time to plant your tetties out!*[15]

Miss A. M. Trump of Broadclyst, Devon, tells of the old squire of her village ('rather a stern old gentleman, white-bearded, so clearly in my memory') who 'as soon as he heard the cuckoo for the first time in the year, would stop his man, no matter what he was doing and tell him to put in the French beans at once!',[16] linking practicality with the magical reappearance of the bird of summer. Similarly in ancient Rome the arrival of the stork ('when the golden spring reveals the year, And the white bird returns, whom serpents fear') was the planting signal for owners of vineyards.

Not everyone relies upon nature: 'An old lady living opposite us told me that her father used to say, "By the time Genesis is finished reading, my garden should be planted." By the church lectionary, Genesis is started reading on Septuagesima Sunday, usually about the first or second week in February, and is finished about the second week in March—and I suppose that in a good season he could get his garden planted in this time.'[17] In the Ozarks and Kentucky the hundredth day of the year—10 April, or 9 April in leap years—is correct for bean and potato planting,[18] and a correspondent mentions the Grand National steeplechase run at Aintree as a gardeners' reminder around Liverpool, England: 'It is said that roses should be pruned on the Sunday after the Grand National. This was always run on the last Friday in March until the last war; since then it has been run on the last Saturday. Winters must have been colder when the belief developed. Today roses always seem to be ready for pruning much earlier.' Some see Grand National Day itself as correct for both pruning and planting roses.[19]

THE DATE OF EASTER

The twentieth century argues in favour of fixing the date of Easter, as a commercial convenience. Lord Desborough's Bill, debated at Westminster in 1927-8, proposed that Easter be always on the Sunday following the second Saturday in April, but although the Bill reached the statute book it stands suspended pending the sanction of the Christian churches. While from time to time moves have been made to obtain this, at present (1977) Easter is still ruled by the moon.

Easter, a moon festival occurring on the first Sunday after the first full moon falling on or after the vernal equinox on 21 March, was said by the Venerable Bede, one of the most learned of early writers, to take its name from Eostre, the Teutonic goddess of spring, fêted at that season. The Church united Easter and Eostre's feast: William Wood, author of *A Sussex Farmer* (1938), heard a farmworker express the true chronology: 'Ah, Easter Sunday, that's the first Sunday after the first full moon after you put your onions in!' Easter gardening beliefs, now linked with Christianity, are the property of a far older deity.

All Lenten landmarks depend upon Easter's moveability over thirty-five days, which affects the ecclesiastical calendar from Septuagesima until Trinity Sunday. Early or late Easters produce the greatest variation in applicability of beliefs and it is a tribute to its resilience that, after nearly 2,000 years of Christianity, the Old Religion survives so vigorously, affecting not only the prime festival of the Christian church but innumerable gardens also.

In Maryland, ashes scattered round fruit trees on Ash Wednesday, first day of Lent, safeguard the trees from bugs for the whole season, a custom which must have derived from the Roman Catholic practice of burning then the palms used in the Palm Sunday church services of the previous year. In Shropshire onion sowing was customary on Ash Wednesday. At the other end of Lent, on Palm Sunday, a week before Easter Day, onions and leeks are sown in France:

> *Le propre jour de Rameaux,*
> *Sème oignons et poreux.*

A customer in a Gloucestershire seedmerchant's shop, about 1800, wrote of another Palm Sunday belief:

> A circumstance occurring in my presence on Saturday evening last (the 31st of March) brought to my recollection a superstitious notion which I have often heard repeated. A lady . . . requested of a seedsman that she might be furnished with various flower-seeds, 'for,' she added, 'I must not omit sowing them tomorrow.' 'May I inquire,' exclaimed the astonished shopman, 'if there is any particular reasons for you making choice of that day?' 'Yes,' was the answer; 'it is because tomorrow is Palm Sunday, and the advantage to be derived from sowing on that day is, that the flowers will be sure to come double!'

GOOD FRIDAY IN THE GARDEN

It may be said with confidence that the greatest body of gardening lore remembered today revolves round Good Friday, formerly a rare break in the working man's year as well as a holy day. 'Good Friday on most farms (after church in the morning) was a holiday: the gardening year started then.'[20] American gardeners regard Good Friday as the best day to spray fruit trees with insecticides: the day hallows the deed. In Devon anything planted or grafted on Good Friday 'grows goody'. But, as an exception to this widespread confidence, soil in Yorkshire gardens was never disturbed with iron tools then, in remembrance of the use made of iron at the crucifixion (or, some say, of a far older belief placing certain taboos on iron as the metal of Thor). Under the influence of Christianity it came to be believed that soil touched on Good Friday might bleed.

In general, however, gardeners seized their chance. Like those of Palm Sunday, gilliflowers sown at noon precisely on Good Friday, or after sundown, would come double. About 1858 Canon Bingham, presented with a Brompton stock plant from a Dorset cottage garden, was assured proudly that its excellence was due solely to Good Friday planting. In both Germany and North Carolina there was a bonus of variegated flowers. Bearing a blood red spot on its leaves and a seed-pod unwinding into a 'crown of thorns', Calvary clover, which grew beneath the cross, would germinate only if sown on this day. Many flowers share similar associations: the crown imperial forever holds a 'tear-drop' within its bell flowers because it arrogantly refused to bow its head on the original Good Friday.

Few beliefs attach to Easter Saturday, a time of waiting for the resurrection, but Christopher Sansom writes of a Surrey tradition:

In 1954, our old gardener whom we had had at Kennel Moor throughout my life, was due to retire, and for some months we had casual help in the garden, until a new resident gardener came . . . It was at Easter-time in 1955 that my father suggested to the part-time gardener that we assumed that he would want the Easter weekend free from work. He replied that he would like to do the spring sowing of various things on the day following Good Friday 'while the Master's body lay on the ground'.[21]

THE PUZZLE OF PARSLEY

The most persistent of all gardening folklore surrounds parsley. Of 267 letters on gardening beliefs which the writer received while preparing this book, no fewer than 127 mentioned parsley superstitions in some form. A 'lightning plant' of Celtic paganism, parsley enjoys a magical reputation: if boy babies are to be discovered under the gooseberry bush, girls will certainly be found in the parsley patch!: Napoleon's troops sang bawdily round their campfires:

> *'Mongst the parsley she was seen, Jeanne,*
> *Searching for a baby.*

Parsley's connections with sex, death and male and female ascendancy are ancient. The Greeks strewed their tombs with the herb and 'to be in need of parsley' was their description of a patient *in extremis*. Only a few of a hundred variant beliefs can be mentioned. Good Friday plant-ing at the hours of the crucifixion is often recommended for parsley. One gardener wrote:

> I tried several sowings without success until I mentioned the problem to an old gardener. He told me to plant parsley seed on Good Friday between the hours of twelve and three. This I did and the results were fantastic—a rich, thick growth of the most lovely parsley . . . But the following year I planted it *before* Good Friday and nothing came up. The next year I again planted *on* Good Friday: another lovely crop resulted which served not only us but the neighbours around . . .[22]

A man's sexual powers are believed to be strongly affected by parsley, and in Gloucestershire villages parsley wine is an esteemed aphrodisiac. The plant also influences, and is influenced by, women. The master of the house must quickly uproot over-lush parsley in his garden lest girls only be born in his family: if a woman of child-bearing age sows parsley she may expect to be pregnant before it germinates.[23] Many say that parsley should be set only by a woman and that as she flourishes or languishes this life-index will do likewise:[24] others assert that it thrives only 'where the old grey mare is the better horse' or if sown by the *true* head of the house—whether male or female. Similar superstitions attach to other herbs: 'If the sage-bush thrives and grows, the master's not master and he knows!' is the discouraging assessment of the English Midlands. As late as 1948 a North Oxfordshire man was dis-covered furtively chopping down a too-flourishing sage-bush . . .

Herb lore is too wide a subject to be fully discussed here but it is interesting to speculate in passing on why herbs, the most inconspicuous and muted of plants, should carry a seemingly disproportionate burden of folk beliefs. Such lore must surely have originated in earliest times (the wild thymes, mints and sages are scarcely less effective than cultivated forms) when the indispensability of herbs in cooking and preserving food and in medicine became plain. Possibly this domestic pre-eminence in kitchen and stillroom led naturally to the selection of herbs as indicators in matters of domestic politics, birth and death; reputations which have lasted until the present day.

Mrs Ivy Hysted expresses more of the ambivalent humour surrounding parsley—this time supporting the man of the house:

> My old dad said, 'Parsley won't grow where the *missis* is master.' There's no doubt at all about who is boss in our particular set-up; we've got plants of parsley all over the garden! My husband has even planted some in the flower borders, where it looks lovely with its dark green curled leaves . . . I think he plants it to remind me who *is* master! It certainly thrives in our garden—but I pretend not to notice![25]

To deter Satan, who controls seed-growth, some pour boiling water over freshly-sown parsley seed: Miss Elizabeth Reynolds of Upton Snodsbury, Worcestershire, tried this and writes:

> That first border was a huge success and ever since, parsley has grown for me like nothing else . . . growth has been so prolific that I have even resorted to taking bags of it to the fishmonger in Worcester and have used it for parsley wine.[26]

Good Friday planting—on a day when the devil is powerless—eliminates the journey which parsley is otherwise obliged to make, nine (two, three or seven) times to Satan before it begins to grow. 'Seeds go to hell to make their obedience to their Master before they come up for you.'[27] (Indeed, it may forget to come back at all, that is, to germinate.) Some advise *two* sowings for the devil and *one* for the gardener.[28] Tardy germination explains all these beliefs. Mechanical problems abound: in Maryland and Louisiana ominous parsley seed must never be hand-sown but rather blown from a bible or gatepost onto the seedbed; in Texas it is scattered on the kitchen floor and tossed casually onto the garden with the dust. Only then will it grow.[29]

Transplanting parsley is perilous to life and limb. Some avoid it yet. Miss W. R. Bush of Guernsey writes of friends there, about 1906:

The gardener was told to transplant some parsley; he flatly refused to do so saying it would cause a death in the family. His employer dismissed this as nonsense and transplanted the parsley himself. Within three months both he and his baby daughter were dead . . . as a family we have never forgotten this and none of us would ever transplant parsley.[30]

Immemorial disaster looms over the parsley transplanter. The Pennsylvanian Germans say that he himself will die, though some regard Good Friday as a protective day, the only time when parsley may be moved with safety. Parsley's strong link with death is hard to account for, but the plant's bifurcated reputation (its associations with babies, sex and fertility are just as lively) is a sure indication of the antiquity of the beliefs surrounding it. (Elder is another capable of both favouring and striking.) At the parsley patch life and death draw close together and, since parsley beds are a source of infant life, to uproot the plant perhaps not only betokens, but absolutely causes, death?

POTATOES AND GOOD FRIDAY

Potato planting is another Good Friday ritual. The Christian veneer is deceptive for the crowded influences bearing on this choice of date are entirely pagan in origin. Something must be said of each. Moon planting (Easter is a moon festival when moon beliefs are to the fore) ordains that root crops be planted in the wane for best results. This doctrine *usually* applies to Good Friday, when, more often than not, the moon is waning. But occasionally full moon occurs on Good Friday itself, or Good Friday falls upon the day before full moon. Thus from time to time (and inevitably if the 'plant potatoes on Good Friday' injunction is strictly obeyed year by year) it is necessary to break the rule and to plant *on* full moon day, or on the day *preceding* full moon. But this need not destroy the theory for we may see here a last flicker of ancient prohibition: to ignore a taboo thus, with deliberation on an appointed day, enhances its general strength.

Riding alongside and providing a further rationale for potato planting on 'full moon' or 'coming to full' Good Fridays is the broader belief that the moon's increase stimulates all plant growth, root or leaf. And the Kolisko finding that planting forty-eight hours before full moon is beneficial to roots as well as leafy crops may also be relevant.

These beliefs all impinge, to some degree, on Good Friday potato planting: the practising gardener may take his choice.

Pagan planting beliefs concerning the cosmic mystery of winter and spring were taken under the cloak of Christianity and became heavily veiled with Christian symbolism. The process cannot have been rapid: even in the eleventh century Canute the Great passed laws prohibiting the people from worshipping 'the sun, moon, sacred groves and woods...'. The ecclesiastical authorities were to pronounce such decrees again and again, in vain. But gradually the transition took hold: today Christian imagery dominates Easter potato planting and is straightforward enough. Seemingly dead tubers are laid in the soil in the confident expectation of their resurrection in imitation of Christ.

With the coming of Christianity it is probable that the day of preparation for Eostre's feast under the Old Religion (marked by sacrifice) became Good Friday. Then the power of Satan (the transmogrified chthonic god of the pre-Christian religion who controls everything beneath the earth) was held to be suspended. It is probable that the pagans, with due ceremony, had ritually curbed the authority of their god of the underworld to permit seed-sowing under the White Goddess's protection. Too intransigent a chthonic power would, after all, halt all husbandry. In the Christian context Satan was rendered impotent through the sacrifice of the crucifixion; doubtless the Old God's impotence was no less effectively contrived through pagan mechanisms.

Many parallels have been drawn between Christianity and the paganism it essayed to replace. Christ is matched by the sun god: during excavations beneath the high altar of St Peter's Church in Rome in the nineteen-fifties an early Christian mosaic was found portraying Christ as the Sun God Helios driving his chariot across the sky, cloak flying, a rayed nimbus behind his head. Early Christians believed (a shadow survives today in Easter sunrise services) that the sun danced on Easter morning. Gaps between old and new were easily bridged. At Eostre's festival pagans expressed their delight in the renewed growth of vegetation after harsh winter and their confidence that new life rose from the dark soil. 'Make sacrifice each year to sovereign Ceres, when the grass is green and glad,' wrote Virgil. Christians were to interpret

F

these emotions through the rolling away of the stone—personifying winter—from the tomb, and in Christ's resurrection.

There are many clues as to the history of these beliefs. The White Goddess or Earth Mother, the essential feminine principle (of whom Eostre is one manifestation), is discernible in all the pantheons of the primitive peoples who carried agriculture and their fertility religion from the Mediterranean across Europe. The megalithic architecture of New Stone Age Britain (and even more so that of Europe) points to a cult of the great goddess mating with a male consort god, her son or lover, who died each harvest-time and was triumphantly reborn amid ceremonies each spring. Thus was the fecundity of plants and animals and the blessing of agriculture secured. This religion was to be set aside for the new male sky god, the first of the Fathers in Heaven, brought by belligerent Bronze Age invaders: but there is ample evidence that the Earth Mother was never forgotten by her followers. Her trees (elder and hawthorn come notably to mind) retain arcane virtue in country eyes, and until a hundred years ago 'corn-dollies', images of the goddess made from corn-stalks or husks, were essential charms to secure the continuance of harvest. Despite changes in husbandry, inscrutable old gods, the Earth Mother one of their company, still brood, unmoved, over the countryside. The rural dean of *Akenfield*, the Suffolk village portrayed by Ronald Blythe in 1972, decided, after a twenty-year ministry, that the real controlling force for his parishioners was fatalism, joined with divinities of plants, sky and water: these he felt were the true rulers, despite outward Christianity. Villagers were more closely linked than they knew with propitiatory practices in the fields.[31]

How easily the potato would have fitted into the Earth Mother's ageless cult of dark earth and rebirth, lately glossed by Christianity! No wonder potatoes were so enthusiastically received when they reached England in the sixteenth century. It was a reception on two levels: for a wholesome, easily-cultivated staple food, and for a vegetable whose planting gave free rein to immemorial emotions, ritual practices and homage to old gods. Nevertheless potatoes joined the cult late in the day: although cultivated for thousands of years by the Indians of Central and South America, potatoes did not arrive in Europe until the Elizabethan period. John Gerard in his *Herbal* (1597) was the first to describe them, saying that his plants had come from Virginia 'to grow and prosper in my garden as in their native country'. But potatoes were not grown in Virginia at that time and it has been conjectured that when Francis Drake brought the Virginia settlers back to Plymouth in July 1586, potatoes came with them, perhaps from Cartagena or Hispaniola, inadvertently mixed with Virginian plants. The Indians probably observed moon planting requirements and the beliefs may well have arrived as part of potato husbandry. Elizabethan gardeners were much attracted to astrology and receptive to magical ideas, had these been presented to them with an exotic new vegetable.

Potatoes have a further association with the true pagan character of Easter. The Elizabethans were familiar with the sweet potato (*Ipomoea Batatas*) imported from Spain and Portugal with the highest aphrodisiac reputation depending on its phallic shape. It was to this potato that Shakespeare referred: 'Let the sky rain potatoes,' said Falstaff. But the newly-introduced vegetable *Solanum tuberosum*, the familiar potato of today's vegetable garden, was also of sexual shape, suggesting testicles rather than penis, and quickly took over some of the old aphrodisiac lore of its predecessor. Easter derives from a festival of spring fertility and the strong link between it and the potato could well be, at least in part, aphrodisiac. But whether this is the case or not, the sturdy conviction in Britain that Good Friday is the right and proper day to plant potatoes can be no older than 390 years. Among superstitions it is a neophyte.

Some of course argue that 'spud day' was celebrated for practical reasons alone. In Sussex, Norfolk and other counties this view could be supported, particularly in the last century, by the farmers' customary loan of ploughs and horses to their men to prepare their potato plots after church on Good Friday.

Whatever its beginnings, Good Friday potato planting holds firm in the minds, if not in the actions, of modern gardeners. Nowadays more attribute it to their fathers or say evasively 'It's always done round here' than admit to practising it wholeheartedly themselves. Nevertheless most gardeners questioned at random about Easter beliefs waste little time in bringing both potato and parsley planting into the conversation. These are superstitions near the surface.

One correspondent felt it noteworthy that her father, a strict

Methodist, who otherwise carried out only the most essential chores on Good Friday, would garden on that day.[32] This suggests the survival of a ritual of some seniority. Such plantings are sometimes held to benefit all others of that year: obvious magic lies in a conviction from Riceville, Iowa, 'that a token hill or two of potatoes must at all costs be set on Good Friday, even if the gardener has to chop his way through frosted ground to do so'; and more than a little communal ritualism clings to Easter gardening: 'What are you doing for Easter?' 'Get into the garden!' Everyone does it: it is right. But above all symbolism still suffuses the work:

> When I, a High Anglican, was courted by a practising Methodist, knowing nothing of their ways of worship, I asked him what he did on Good Friday. I was a little taken aback to be told 'Plant potatoes!'. But when you think about it, I wonder if it isn't symbolic, to put a dead-looking thing into the earth, knowing that it will come up again.[33]

Older allegiances to Sol, the sun god, must surely underlie the remarkable instruction of an 85-year-old farm-worker in south Norfolk, who said that potatoes should be 'sown on Good Friday, *with the sprout facing the rising sun*'.[34] Another Norfolk belief (the triumph of hope over experience) proclaims that potatoes planted on Good Friday will be ready to eat on Whit-Sunday,[35] and a 'feast and fair days' reminder is recalled by a Durham miner's daughter: 'My late Dad planted his potatoes on Good Friday and took them up on Durham Miners' Gala Day in July.'[36]

A few crops other than dominant parsley and potatoes receive Easter mentions. In North Carolina snap beans are set on Good Friday morning: if sown in the afternoon their flowers will drop off;[37] and in *A Book of Exmoor*, F. J. Snell tells how a new incumbent, mystified by the poor attendance at his Good Friday church service, was told that his parishioners were busy planting their beans so that the shoots would appear above ground on Easter morning!

THE GREEN OF MAY

May is the month of Maia, another aspect of the White Goddess, whose blossom is the white hawthorn flower of the hedgerows: she presides over spring growth: Guernseymen say:

> *Sème tes concombres en Mars,*
> *Tu n'airas qu'faire de pouque nide sac;*
> *Sème-les en Avril, tuen airas ûn petit;*
> *Mé, j'les semerai en Mai,*
> *Et j'en airai pûs que té.*

> *Sow your cucumbers in March,*
> *You will need neither bag nor sack;*
> *Sow them in April, you will have a few;*
> *I will sow mine in May,*
> *And I will have more than you!*

Weeds are a less welcome part of the spring surge. Correct destruction ensures success:

> *Cut a thistle in May, he'll be there next day,*
> *Cut a thistle in June, he'll come again soon,*
> *Cut him in July and he's sure to die!*[38]

Pulling weeds in advance of the diminutory influence of the summer solstice is a waste of time:

> *Who weeds in May*
> *Throws all away!*

but 'to cut a foul weed on or near the twenty-second of June, in the afternoon and at full moon' means its certain end, for the plant has been attacked at the height of, at once, the year, the day and the moon's cycle.

May is apple blossom month but in Devon they say that gardening is safest when Franklin's nights are past. 'If there were a warm spell in early May the mother of a Devon friend would suggest putting out the bedding plants, but her old gardener always said, "Wait until after Franken nights."' The devil often blasts the orchards with late frost: sometimes on 19, 20 and 21 May; sometimes 20, 21 and 22; sometimes for three days from 17 ending on 19 May (St Dunstan's Day, this saint being an alternative villain). St Franklin or Franken set up as a brewer and to safeguard his sales sold his soul to the devil in return for frosts to destroy the apple blossom—and thus, cider. In Kent St Franklin is a *cider-maker* who arranged a similar attack on young *hops*. The story may vary but the three cold nights, if not actual frost, nearly always occur.[39] Round Mont St-Michel, Normandy, on similar dates, apple

blossom is laid on the altar of the Blessed Virgin Mary to solicit divine
protection for the orchards.

May 1, though heralded by Walpurgis Night, the feast of witches,
and therefore of dubious reputation, was regarded by bolder gardeners
as an auspicious opportunity to bring occult forces to their aid. In
Illinois watermelons sown before sunrise on May morning will never
be attacked by bugs (the beneficial aspects of an otherwise minatory
day could be exploited). The calendar changes of 1752 destroyed the
pastoral, if not the magical, traditions of May Day; now leaves and
flowers were backward on 1 May. But a trace of the old May Day
power is still detectible and dates about Old May Day, 12, 13 and 14
of May, are widely recommended for bean-planting: 'An old man
once told me that after the first day of spring, March 21, you can sow
any kind of seed with success, except kidney beans, which should be
set about May 12,' writes a Lincolnshire correspondent.[40] In West
Surrey, country people plant runner beans on 13 May;[41] in Shropshire
on 14 May; in Massachusetts the legendary 'trout bean', traditional
ingredient of pioneer 'pork and beans', is sown about 15 May.[42] After
1752 some May fairs continued on May Day, Old Style, and today
their dates still figure in planting reminders.

> *Twelfth of May, Stow Fair Day,*
> *Sow your kidney beans today*

is the axiom of the ancient horse-fair held in the Cotswold streets of
Stow-on-the-Wold.[43] And a gardener from Wendover, Buckinghamshire, writes: 'I was told that runner beans should be planted on the
day the fair comes here, 13 May.'[44] Round Waddesdon, says Cecil
Atkins, typifying many, very local reminders, 'Ashendon Feast Day',
the festival of the parish church high on the limestone ridge, is proper
for bean-planting.

WHITSUN AND GOOSEBERRY SHOWS

The gooseberry, grown in English gardens since the reign of Henry
VIII and in the United States from the earliest years of settlement, holds
a venerable place among soft fruits. In Sussex it is still customary for
country families to enjoy the first tart green gooseberries of the season

in Whitsun puddings. A 'la Paintecoûte, les grouïsiaux se goûtent' ('green gooseberries are at perfection at Whitsuntide') is a Guernsey saying, applied irrespectively of Whitsun's changing date.

In the north of England especially, gooseberry shows were, and to a lesser extent still are, great events, dedicated to the presentation of giant fruits. The nineteenth-century annual, *The Manchester Gooseberry Register*, recorded shows by the hundred, with weights of the winners of such favourite prizes as sugar-tongs, corner cupboards and copper tea-kettles. At Egton Bridge, Yorkshire, gooseberries have been lovingly tended for over two and a half centuries and there the Old Gooseberry Society, founded in 1800, holds the Old Gooseberry Show on the first Tuesday of August each year. The society's code is immutable: no new member may compete with bushes belonging to another member (unless of the same family), and transfers of bushes are carried out under the strict eye of committee members. Favourite varieties shown are Lord Kitchener (hairy), Lord Derby (flushed with pink), Fascination and Prince Charles.[45] In 1952 Tom Ventress showed a legendary berry weighing nearly two ounces. In the 1840s, villagers of Hartwell, Buckinghamshire, where lively gooseberry shows were held under the patronage of the Lee family of Hartwell House, remembered sitting up all night in the garden as show day approached to minister to the swelling fruit. (In 1841 the four winning berries weighed 98dwts 4grs.) A circular pan of water lay about the stem of each bush, gooseberries were drastically thinned and as the water evaporated in the hot sun 'you could fairly see 'em grow'.

Even the names of the gooseberries favoured in the middle years of the nineteenth century have a poetry of their own: American gardeners grew Ironmonger, Red Champagne, Red Walnut, Green Globe, Golden Drop, Sulphur, Yellow Champagne, Conqueror and Large Crystal: English gardeners liked the personal touch of the creator as part of the fruit's name: Leicester's Smoker, Pilkington's Farmer, Prophet's Diadem, Becket's Bravo, Wilkinson's Oyster Girl, Eardlay's Hannah, Shingler's Edna and Walton's Annie—a cluster of sweethearts and wives.

Violating the mystically holy Ascension Day by as much as walking through the garden—let alone working in it—means that the garden 'will not be any count'. In North Germany there is a dispensation for one crop, for runner beans may be planted while Ascension Day bells are ringing. But the seeds must be set no deeper than one inch because 'they want to hear the church bells on Sundays'—and will thus flourish.[46] Holy Thursday rain is curative (and makes, for example, an excellent eye lotion): a Pennsylvanian gardener said in 1973 that a splash of this 'magic rain' added to the watering-can gave seedlings a promising start in life.

ABOUT MIDSUMMER DAY

Celebration of the summer solstice, about 21 June, was transferred by the early Church to St John the Baptist's Day on 24 June. After 1752 Old Midsummer Day, 6 July, retained some charm, and even 75 years later William Hone reported in his *Every-Day Book*:

> This Day is still marked in our almanacs, on account of its being adhered to, in a few places, as a 'good old day' of the 'good old time'.

In Britain, apart from a few fairs still held on 6 July, Old Midsummer is now forgotten, but Kentuckians, who preserve many traditions, say:

> *Plant cucumber seed on 6 July,*
> *You'll have cucumbers, wet or dry!*

Understandably enough, Americans have often come to attach such beliefs to *4 July*, a day of superior importance; but the planting of beans and turnips so often advised for that date is in fact of far earlier origin than 1776.

BLESSING THE APPLES

On 15 July 1870 a Huntingdonshire farm labourer told his vicar:

> I shall get a few o' them codlins for a dumplin' for my Sabbath dinner. I never taste an apple till the Sabbath after St Swithin's for there's an old saying:
> *Till St Swithin's day be past,*
> *The apples be not fit to taste.*

He was referring to the ancient notion that without the 'blessing' of rain on 15 July, apples are worthless; as another old lady added: 'We must have rain tomorrow, sir, to *christen the apples* . . . if the apples don't get christened, they comes to nothing.' When the new cathedral was completed at Winchester in AD970, St Swithin's bones were moved indoors from their former position in the churchyard: he, objecting, 'wept'—so effectively that rain on St Swithin's Day is followed by rain, more or less, for the next forty days, which benefits apples.

Some say (with an eye to the old calendar) that the blessing is performed by St James, whose day is 25 July. In Cheshire the small, gaily-striped, red and yellow 'Sainjam' apple matured so early as to be ready for the saint's feast; and 'We have a pear too, which, on account of its juiciness, rejoices in the elegant soubriquet of *Slobberchops*,' wrote an informant in *Notes and Queries* in 1874. In fact the customary growth spurt of mid-July swells the green waxen fruit with or without saintly assistance.

Before uncertain dates and seasons intervened a few years ago, mystical favours were invoked in the Michigan cherry orchards with 'blessing the blossoms',[47] and when Vaughan Cornish visited the Japanese orchards about 1910 he found that there too cherry blossom had religious significance—although in Japan it was more widely associated with spiritual immanence in all nature, rather than with specific personages.

In the Ozarks, we are told, for at least one hundred years St James's Day has been considered a reliable choice for the planting of turnips, regardless of moon, signs or weather:

> *Plant 25 July*
> *Wet or dry!*

FALL FAIRS AND FLOWER SHOWS

Amid high piled golden corn and scarlet apples, the rich and spicy scents of damp crushed grass and summer flowers, gardening reputations have been made or broken at the 'fall fairs' of America and flower shows of Britain. As a custom, flower shows are said to have been brought from France in the seventeenth century by Huguenot refugees. Some, like the gooseberry shows, revolve round a theme: apples, pumpkins, onions, fuchsias, dahlias, chrysanthemums—in the early nineteenth century, auricula shows were important in North of England life. Others have seasonal accents—spring, summer, autumn— or a partiality among exhibitors—old age pensioners, policemen or postmen. In addition, of course, there are countless thousands of general shows. Junior classes for collections of pressed wild flowers, and others for home-made wines, honey, preserves, cookery, flower arrangements and handicrafts are traditional, as much as those for flowers, fruit and vegetables.

In America and Canada people think nothing of travelling upwards of fifty miles to their fall fair, a magnet for the neighbourhood rivalled only by Christmas, and a last chance to meet distant friends before winter sets in. To enlarge upon the occasion we have the account of N. Ludy of Springtown, Arkansas, who in 1888 confided triumphantly to the W. Atlee Burpee seed company: 'I have just been to the district fair at Rogers, Arkansas, and have taken the premium on onions—the largest grown in four counties. I raised two bushels of onions from one ounce of Mammoth Pompeii seed . . . had several specimens that weighed $1\frac{1}{2}$ pounds, and we had had a bad drought this season.' (Nevertheless he fell far behind George H. Slaymaker of Atkinson, Nebraska, who managed a five-pound six-ounce giant from the same seed.)

Typical too of their period are the memories of Charlotte M. Wood, daughter of the head gardener at Totteridge House, Buckinghamshire, about 1900. Hothouse cucumbers were her father's speciality and for weeks before the High Wycombe Flower Show each grew within a paraffin lamp glass, that it might emerge rod-straight and perfect for the competition. On the day before the show unblemished peas picked lightly, their waxy bloom untarnished, were packed in boxes lined with cotton wool and, a forbidden but enhancing stroke, each carrot and potato was anointed with a little butter. Sweetpeas, never fewer than five superb blooms to each straight long stem, were laid with the vegetables in the little donkey cart for carriage to the town hall. Vegetables were displayed against black velvet and sweetpeas meticulously set six to a glass: the final composition was the 'Floral Group'—brilliant, many-coloured nemesias, blood-red and lemon snapdragons in glowing rings, rising to a centrepiece of deep blue, sky blue and purple delphiniums and larkspurs, with green and silver foliage intervening, like a soaring crown reaching nearly to the roof of the hall.

HALLOWE'EN AND PUMPKINS

Hallowe'en, *Samhain* or Winter's Eve in the Celtic calendar, a 'junction night' between seasons when witches set spells, was a turning point in the year: in Ireland, fruit left on the trees after *Samhain* is still reckoned to be contaminated by the 'púca', or spirits, and unfit to eat. It was a night for disguises, mischief, turnip lanterns and begging 'soulers': bonfires blazed, at first to drive away witches, later, under Christianity, to light souls from purgatory.

North America enthusiastically took up Hallowe'en customs, quickly replacing the traditional turnips with pumpkins, carved with eyes, nose and grinning mouth, with, for fullest effect, a candle burning within, and carried on a stick or set outside the house. Today crowds of begging children fill the streets, calling 'trick or treat', and house-holders disobliging enough to withhold a gift of candy or money are likely to find their garbage cans overturned by morning. Pumpkin cultivation by gardeners is a traditional ritual and every seed catalogue in America offers Hallowe'en varieties. Burpee suggests 'Big Max', which grows to one hundred pounds or better, as 'perfect for making huge Jack o' Lanterns': in Canada Stokes Seeds Ltd have, among others, 'Spookie' seeds; and of another favourite, 'Jack o' Lantern', Dominion Seed House say 'specially developed ... for Hallowe'en use'.

Pumpkin competitions are increasingly popular in North America. Weights vary greatly with variety and climate. Genetically pumpkins, squashes and marrows are closely related, much crossed and hard to differentiate: the confusion is well pointed in Burpee's 1888 catalogue where under 'Pumpkin' the 'new Golden Marrow' is described as 'one of the best yellow pumpkin pie pumpkins' and under 'Squash' Boston Marrow is 'this new squash'. Records are constantly broken but in 1975 Mark Coon of Ashville, Ohio, was named as the world-record holder with a Hungarian Mammoth Squash weighing 378 pounds. (In 1888 Burpee was offering the endearingly-named pumpkin 'Genuine Mammoth, or True Potiron, also called King of the Mammoths'.) Pumpkin seed improves with age up to the magic number of seven years. By tradition old seed produces more female flowers and size is said to be inherited on the female side.

The greatest display of giant pumpkins is to be seen at the October Pumpkin Festival at Circleville, Ohio, 'Pumpkin Capital of the World Since 1903', where mountains of piled pumpkins, squashes and other gourds, corn and vegetables, in glowing autumn shades of orange, yellow and cream, line Main Street.

WINTER WEATHER SIGNS

The gardener's year is almost done and he contemplates the winter ahead. Dogwood days were prophetic, if he can recall them, for abundant spring blossom signals a cold winter to come. Heavy swags of shell-pink dog-roses or white hawthorn flowers in the hedgerows of early summer, late blooming cherry trees or lilacs or a handsome crop of hedgerow berries of holly and redhaw, everywhere portend hard weather. English gardeners say:

> *Onion skin, very thin,*
> *Mild winter coming in;*
> *Onion skin thick and tough,*
> *Coming winter cold and rough.*

New England gardeners substitute an apple-skin and American Indians believe that if sweet corn is thicker husked than usual, making cleaning irksome, hard weather will surely follow. Wiltshire people see an omen in a field-mouse's nest, for if she builds with the entrance to the south a severe winter is to be expected, if to the north, much rain. In the United States the katydid, a small grasshopper-like insect, is a most dependable herald of the weather; in August it calls 'six weeks to frost, six weeks to frost', a warning which is valid three years out of four. Promptly six weeks after the first rasp of the katydid's wings is heard the cold finger of coming winter is felt.[48]

4

WITCHCRAFT AND THE SUPERNATURAL

Today gardeners live in a climate of rationality. Plant diseases perplex for no longer than it takes to telephone the county horticultural adviser: we have explanations, if not always remedies. This state has come about only recently. According to Pliny the evil eye was so seriously regarded in ancient Rome that laws were enacted against injury to crops through incantation, excantation or fascination; and even one hundred years ago fears that such afflictions arose from supernatural causes could be very real indeed. The ancient dread may linger yet. In 1974 an elderly correspondent from Chesterfield, Derbyshire, concluded a letter to the writer with the words: 'Please don't mention my name: there's some round here as isn't too particular—I don't want them *looking* at *my* garden.' 'Some persons' eies are very offensive ... there is *aliquid divinum* in it, more than anyone thinks,' wrote John Aubrey in the seventeenth century, showing proper respect for the possessors of a mysterious gift, who could make their uncomfortable powers felt in many effective ways.

EYE, VOICE AND HAND

At Wherstead, Suffolk, about 1880, a row of promising plum trees, suddenly languishing, was said to have been 'cursed' by a local wizard, heard muttering maledictions as he stumped by. The exercise of the disagreeable endowment of the evil eye might directly benefit a witch's pocket and possessions: in the 1890s a Sussex witch found that when poking round village gardens, she had but to whisper to watching

children: 'What a fine crop of plums your mother has, dearies,' for the
tree's alarmed owner to send her immediately a basket of the choicest
fruit. To omit this precaution risked the blasting of the tree.

Some unfortunates exercised their gifts without intention. The 'fast-
ing glance', bestowed in early morning when the perpetrator's stomach
was empty, was particularly destructive. A Yorkshireman, aware of the
venom of his eye, killed his own pear tree rather than allow his glance
to fall on passers-by: 'It wor some years back a maast flourishing tree,'
said a neighbour. 'Ivvry morning, as soon as he first oppans the door,
that he may not cast his e'e on onny yan passin' by, he fixes his een o'
that pear-tree, and ye plainly see how it's deed way.' Thomas Hardy,
the poet and novelist, fearing sightseers, fostered a thick hedge of
choice trees round his garden at Max Gate, Dorchester; but despite the
best attention some trees never thrived and a local white witch explained to Hardy that this was because he glanced at them every
morning from the window before breakfast.[1] Perhaps the thinking behind such ideas had a shred of logic: the amusing 1920s toy of the
'Lookatmeter' was said to demonstrate the scientific fact that the human
eye *does* radiate a measurable amount of energy. The slightest glance
was found to deflect the instrument's sensitive plate.

In many countries to point at an object is regarded as unlucky; the
gesture may too easily mask a curse. In Louisiana to point at unripe
fruit with the index finger of the right hand causes it to fall prematurely:
in Maine a daffodil so treated will not bloom.[2] Anticipation of harvest
is universally imprudent and no old-timer dreams of counting the fruit
on a tree or the peas in a pod, lest dark forces be alerted to attack and
the crop fail.

Garden spells are diverse indeed. In Ireland the belief is found that
infertility—an inert state—can be inflicted upon a neighbour's garden
by secretly depositing in it a 'dead' object, to destroy luck and crop. An
egg, boiled potato, hearth ashes or piece of meat, for example, turning
up unexpectedly in the garden, points to witchcraft. In 1974 Fred
Carter of Mullingar, County Westmeath, Ireland, told the writer of a
curious experience bearing on this superstition:

> I came to Ireland in 1949 and bought a small farm. I was amused one day
> when an old man came to my house full of trouble. He was supposed to be
> 84 at the time . . . he was positive that a curse had been put on his potato

crop, for undamaged eggs had turned up in the drills, as he dug the first new potatoes of the season. Eggs in the drill were a sure sign that someone with a grudge had deposited them out of spite.

I tried to assure him that it meant no such thing, but he would not listen. For days he could be seen from my house going carefully over the crop doing untold damage in his efforts to remove the offending eggs. I tried to explain . . . in those days hens ran on free range and eggs were laid daily in the cowstalls and mangers of the farm. The cows were cleaned out every morning after milking and the straw and manure carted to the manure heap outside the yard. A forkful of straw and manure would be lifted without damaging the eggs and when thrown on the dung heap they were still protected. Spontaneous heating of the heap slowly cooked the eggs and they remained preserved until spring, when they were hard as rocks. Manure and eggs were thrown into the potato drills and covered over unseen. Ten weeks later the curse was revealed! Nothing would turn this man's mind and he insisted that he was right even when I went to his garden later in the year when he was harvesting the crop—which was good. He still had curses, he said, and the potatoes would not keep through the winter. I gave up!

Maurice Burton, the nature writer, added to possible explanations when he wrote in 1974 of pulling up a large foxglove which had finished flowering. Its roots formed a clump about nine inches across, and as it left the ground a hen's egg, still fairly fresh, was exposed, although the nearest laying hens were over one hundred yards away, and the foxglove had been in place for nearly two years. Mr Burton wrote that it was nothing unusual for those digging potatoes to unearth one egg after another spread over the whole potato patch. Circumstantial evidence—backed by American research—points to rats laying up eggs in individual food hoards, as carriers.[3] But the whole phenomenon is quite mysterious enough to lend substance to the ancient belief in 'cursing by eggs'. The 'spell' may be a mere accident, but it is no less dreaded for that.

Sometimes spells are not mysteries at all but are publicly enacted before anxious victims. Mrs Isabel Spradley of Van Buren, Arkansas, told of an old woman of her neighbourhood who openly laid a spell on a neighbour's tomato patch, drawing a circle in the dust, marking a cross and spitting in the centre of the cross. No dealer would consider buying the tomatoes, she remembered.

WEEDS AND STONES: MORE CURSES

Until the last century some gardeners took the philosophical view that it was a waste of time to battle with weeds at all. 'They spring eternal from the ground itself, not at all necessarily from the seeds of parent weeds,' was the comfortable philosophy: the ground had been cursed by the Almighty for man's disobedience and 'it has therefore ever borne, and will ever continue to bear, for the punishment of the husbandman . . . thistles and poppies and speargrass' (speargrass is one of the multifarious names for couchgrass). It was almost rebelliously impious to attempt to clear the ground.[4] Yellow flowering groundsel grew where a witch had paused to urinate; old Cambridgeshire Fenmen discerning this evidence in their gardens derived angry satisfaction from wrenching the weed out with an oath and ending the mischief. In Essex, the tallest thistle of any group was the 'devil's thistle' and under his particular protection: its stalk would make an excellent walking-stick for a wizard. In parts of Ireland couchgrass, docks and thistles were regarded as positively helpful: they 'kept the crop warm'.

In certain soils, stones rise to the surface in seemingly never-ending quantities every spring, generating a belief, lively until recent years, that stones 'grow' from 'motherstone', 'breeding-stone' or 'quick-rock' (from the Anglo-Saxon *cwiccan*, 'to make alive'). In Cheshire about 1895 a labourer, asked by a member of a shooting party what a local stone was made of, replied: 'They bean't *made*, sir, they grows.' 'How do you mean *grow*?' 'All the same as taturs grows'; although he did admit that once out of the ground a stone, like a potato, could grow no more, which accounted for the stability of paving-stones.[5]

Ground where a crime has been committed or blood spilled remains ever barren or carries marked crops. An orchard on the site of the Battle of Evesham, fought in Worcestershire in 1265, produced the so-called 'Bloody Pear', with commemorative red-streaked flesh: another pear-tree near Ellesmere, Shropshire, bore red-streaked fruit, because, it was said, a woman had murdered her daughter and buried the body beneath the tree. An apple tree at West Farms, Connecticut, bears fruit with a red globule at the centre, recalling the murder of a pedlar beneath its branches; and rhododendrons in Mast Swamp,

Above, plants enjoying a rendition of Bach's *Minuet in G* at Marty Sussman's flower shop, Montreal, 1975. *Right*, for best results, pruning should be done while the moon is waxing.

Above, a tense moment at Egton Bridge Old Gooseberry Show, Yorkshire. *Below*, F. W. Greenslade of Tunbridge Wells, winner of the Royal Horticultural Society Lindley Medal, with his 'Charm' chrysanthemum, 1973.

Connecticut, show blood-red hearts on the anniversary of the massacre of the Poquetchiet Indians.[6] A patch of ground in the farm garden at Godley Green, Cheshire, was observed to grow nothing; when it was finally dug over late in the nineteenth century human bones were found and reverently buried, but the curse endured and the land remained bare, although garden plants were flourishing all round it.

ORCHARD DENIZENS

From earliest times the orchard has been invested with its own accustomed divinities. The Romans revered Pomona, goddess of fruit-trees and fruit, and set up images in the form of natural tree stumps in their orchards to Bacchus, the personification of the vine and cultivated trees. A representation of Priapus, god of procreation and thus of gardens, carved in figwood, was reckoned to be an effective scarecrow: prudent gardeners remembered to drop an offering of fruit and flowers into his hitched-up gardener's apron, as they left the garden with their baskets of produce.

Among more homely spirits is Lazy Lawrence, a figure of high summer, guarding ripening fruit, whose indolence gave rise to a saying remembered by the gardener at Brightling Place, Sussex, about 1936, when he said of a young helper finding August heat unconducive to weeding: 'He've got St Lawrence on the shoulder.' St Lawrence's Day, 10 August, falls within the dog-days (about 3 July to 11 August) when, it was once thought, the dog-star Sirius's heat combined with that of the sun, to produce days of enervating sultry warmth:

> *Lazy Lawrence let me goo,*
> *Don't hold me summer and winter too,*

is the cry of the saint's perennially languid victims.

The Apple Tree Man resides in the oldest apple tree in the orchard. As a small child in Somerset earlier this century, Ruth Tongue, the folklorist, was shown a venerable apple tree by a school friend with the whispered information that it was the Apple Tree Man. This shadowy orchard god takes other guises: in Hampshire he is the 'colt-pixy' who transfixes orchard thieves; in Yorkshire Awd Goggie, protector of green apples. Fruit has other guardians: in the Isle of Wight the demon

G

'gooseberry wife', in the form of a large hairy caterpillar, is the *genius loci* of the gooseberry patch. Mothers warn children: 'If ye goos out in the garden the gooseberry wife'll be sure to ketch ye'; and to keep children from picking unripe nuts, parents in Canton St Gallen, Switzerland, say: '*S' Haselnussfrauli chimt*'—'The hazelnut lady is coming!'

GARDEN GHOSTS

There are hundreds of garden ghosts. A cottage at Braishfield, Hampshire, is haunted by the ghost of a woman who buried her fortune in the garden but was unable to reveal its whereabouts to her friends before she died. Her phantom has been seen by several living persons and once, when the weather was perfectly calm and clear, tall flowers in a border through which she passed were struck as if by a small cyclone. Dogs passing a certain yew tree from which she emanates pause to growl, although nothing is to be seen. Other treasure-hunting ghosts haunt the gardens of Sykes Lumb farmhouse, Lancashire, and Byewater House, Boldre, in the New Forest, England. A 'boggart' or domestic fairy, who lived on a farm at Hothersall, Ribchester, played many tricks on the household, upset carts, caused butter not to 'take' and turned horses loose, until the knowledgeable farmer contrived to 'lay' the persecutor under a large laurel tree in the farm garden; since it was agreed that the troublemaker could not rise again while the tree lived, the farmer took the trouble to water the laurel often with milk to keep it in good health. (Some incantations for laying boggarts provided for their interment 'so long as hollies are green'; that is, for ever.)

Gardeners return to former scenes. The garden of the Rectory, Pimperne, Dorset, is haunted by the ghosts of an old gardener and his dog who move across the lawn before vanishing. Sussex friends told the writer of an experience about twenty years ago. They maintained a two-acre garden with the help of an elderly local man who had worked for the garden all his life and who had many stories of plantings, wall-buildings and unexpected frosts. He died, still working, at the age of 82 and, while this was a great blow, his employers carried on alone. One day the wife, after a long day pricking-out seedlings, left the potting shed in disarray. To her surprise on the following morning she found everything in perfect order, with seedboxes neatly stacked and sand and earth swept away. She imagined that her husband must have paid an early visit to the shed before leaving for the office, and intended to reprove him for bringing out his old pipe, for she had detected a whiff of tobacco smoke in the shed. But when her husband returned he said he had been late leaving that morning and had certainly not delayed to visit the garden. The state of the shed was never explained but on several occasions during the first summer after the old gardener's death she had similar experiences, finding tools tidily returned to their racks and order restored, with always a touch of tobacco smoke in the air. It was decided that the gardener had not left quite so finally as it had at first seemed.

The Grey House, Batheaston, Somerset, was once the home of a lady who despised hireling gardeners and cared for her garden herself. After her death, at the end of the war, an ex-soldier who had been found a casual gardening job at the Grey House was quickly startled at his weeding by the appearance of a stately lady in purple, clearly angry, who advanced on him shaking her fist: she remained silent but he, assuming that she lived in the house, retreated. Later he heard of the former owner's eccentric dislike of hired gardeners and of her possession of a favourite purple dress.[7]

The apparition of Mrs Baines haunted a house in Chapel Street, Penzance, Cornwall, behind which was a well-stocked orchard where local boys had enjoyed stealing apples. Mrs Baines, annoyed by this intrusion, armed her gardener with an ancient blunderbuss charged with peas and small shot and gave him orders to watch, challenge and fire. But during his two nights of presumed vigilance more fruit was stolen and on the third night Mrs Baines, no doubt hoping to catch her man asleep, herself went into the orchard and shook a tree to bring down fruit. Some said that the gardener was annoyed by her interference, others that he was half-asleep and shot her by mistake; but whatever occurred Mrs Baines was injured, although she was more frightened than hurt and the shot was easily removed by the doctor. But shortly afterwards, perhaps from shock, she died, and the garden became haunted by her ghost, in ancient dress, a lace cap on her powdered hair, lace ruffles on her sleeves and a short cloak over her shoulders, and she was often to be seen walking in the orchard or standing beneath an apple tree, leaning on the gold-headed cane which was ever in her hand.[8]

In Ireland, summerhouses are particularly vulnerable to fairy habitation and haunting. John Phelan told in Lady Gregory's *Visions and Beliefs in the West of Ireland* (1920) that he 'never saw them nor felt them all my life' except when for twelve nights he slept in the garden house to protect the ripening apples. All night he was disturbed by the sounds of fairies scratching, rustling and scraping in the loft above his head. And later 'one night standing by the vinery and the moon shining, on a sudden a wind rose and shook the trees and rattled the glass and the slates, and no wind before, and it stopped as sudden as it came. And there were two bunches of grapes gone, and them that took them took them by the chimney and no other way!'

Diarmuid MacManus has a story of his grandfather's experience in the late 1860s. One night he walked across the orchard to call upon a party of young people dancing in the garden house. It was a pleasant night with the moon a little before full, a light wind and some cloud. As Mr MacManus reached the glade before the apple trees a large wolf-like animal sprang out of the shadows: he waved his arms and tried to shoo it away but at once the creature turned, reared on its hind legs and faced him. It was his own height and *headless*—yet he sensed a glare of deadly loathing. Looking where the head should have been and realizing that he could see the lightly moving apple boughs and clouds behind, he was spellbound, but at last braced himself to make the sign of the cross, when the elemental dropped to all fours and ran away swiftly among the orchard trees.[9]

TREES AND PLANTS OF PRESENCE

Gardeners of all periods have seen the sense of using counter-magic to protect their crops and have shown their respect for trees and plants of presence and reputation. The evidence of their fears and magical applications can be clearly seen today in the hedges and gardens of many old houses in Britain, Ireland and the United States.

Flowers with white blossoms represent, by simple analogy, the beneficent White Goddess in her aspect of spring and regenerative growth. Rowan, hawthorn, dogwood, holly and elder are among those trees which share white flowers and are thus worthy of special treatment (even if a regard tinged with unease). Their red berries also, symbols of blood and therefore of life, are protective against all forces threatening life, including witchcraft and the evil eye.

It is noteworthy that these magical trees all bear flowers or leaves of heavy, rank, even sinister, odour: people are warned, for example, never to sleep beneath an elder for the leaves are reputed to give out a toxic scent which, if inhaled, may send the sleeper into an irreversible coma: in the nineteenth century the sickly scent of hawthorn was identified with the odours of the fever sickroom and of death. Even today many people never permit hawthorn flowers to be brought into the house. These minatory taboos arose from the sacred nature of the tree, revered first by the pagans and later, in mutation, by Christians.

Many Irish gardeners are reluctant to disturb or transplant 'fairy thorns' or 'lone bushes', whitethorns or hawthorns of unusual growth, hoary shape and solitary habit, clearly not planted by the hand of man. Suich fairy trysting places are best avoided, although hedgerow thorns have no significance and may be hacked with impunity. Diarmuid MacManus in *Irish Earth Folk* (1959) wrote of a thorn growing on the 'fary fort' or earthwork of Lis Ard, near his home at Killeaden, County Mayo. Its branches, four feet across and a foot thick, lay flat and round as a grindstone across its trunk. To local people it was a revered fairy tree. In 1851 Mr MacManus's grandfather rashly decided that he would like the tree in his garden, although his neighbours' fears were so real that he was forced to do the work of transplanting unaided. The tree grew—and survives today—but within a few years the transplanter was beset with heavy losses in farm stock and money, and many years later a feeling still persisted locally that for safety's sake the tree should be returned to its original home.

From the Isle of Man comes another story, typical of many such, of a man who lopped a fairy thorn to mend a gap in his fence, pierced his thumb during the work and eventually lost an arm through septicaemia and amputation.

In *Irish Heritage* (1949) Professor Estyn Evans described a beautiful pink-flowered thorn which grew beneath his window at Queen's University, Belfast, casting its shadow into the university senate room. But the story goes that when the university was built, plans had to be altered so that the tree would not be disturbed and, at the time of writing, no gardener bold enough to move or trim the tree had been found. Professor Evans rightly observes that if a garden thorn encircled by austere and level-headed university scientific departments is accorded such respect, how much greater must be the veneration for countryside thorns, the true descendants of the nature deities of Ireland's earliest inhabitants?

In England the world-famous 'Holy Thorn' of Glastonbury, Somerset, which by tradition blooms on Christmas Day (Old Style), was said to have sprung from the thorn-staff of St Joseph of Arimathea: this, thrust into the earth, rooted and bloomed on the day of Christ's birth. (The tree is in fact a *Crataegus monogyna 'Biflora'*, a variety of common hawthorn which blooms in both winter and spring: the belief that the Holy Thorn flowers on Christmas Day is well supported by events.) Various slips have escaped into gardens in both Britain and the United States and a descendant now blooms in the grounds of the National Cathedral, Washington, DC. Disrespectful molesting of such a tree was ill-advised: one holy thorn growing at Redmarley Farm, Acton Beauchamp, Worcestershire, was felled by a farmer exasperated by crowds of sightseers, but he was quickly rewarded: first he broke an arm, then a leg, and finally part of his farmhouse was burned down; all events confidently attributed by the village to a 'judgement'.

It is revealing to see such ancient reputations in their American settings. In the United States the redhaw or hawthorn is as inviolate as any fairy thorn or holy thorn of England and Ireland. In 1923 the redhaw was named the state tree of Missouri, but to far from general approbation. Many older residents in the southern part of the state uneasily viewed the tree as 'sinister', and today still avoid all contact with it, especially (as with the 'Judas tree' and dogwood) when it is in flower.

Trees belonging to a protective goddess must never be handled unnecessarily or irreverently: no one willingly touched growth of such potence, and Christianity, mindful of the strength of pagan taboos, quickly obliged with fresh, acceptable rationales, connected with the birth of Christ or with his crucifixion. Nevertheless the pagan aspects of the trees have never been quite eclipsed and the protective as well as the threatening aspects survive. Such dual reputations are evidence of antiquity: only in later days did deities take on defined and separate character such as Christ and Satan; at first the qualities of good and evil were complementary in the one personage. Farm stock always did well in a field in which a thorn grew and, until the nineteenth century, a sprig of hawthorn gathered on Maundy Thursday or Ascension Day (again combining pagan and Christian beliefs) and hidden in the house-roof was certain to save the household from lightning. Mrs Hayes advises from Dublin: 'Hawthorn among your hedging plants helps to ward off bad fairies!'

In Arkansas the red-stemmed dogwood, especially brilliant in rain, with all the attributes of a tree of the Goddess, like the elder provided the wood for Calvary and was therefore 'cursed by Christ'. Its heavily scented flowers, white with a red spot—a 'drop of blood'—are said by some to resemble the crown of thorns, and many gardeners prefer to avoid this tree during its spring blooming. The American 'Judas tree', or redbud *Cercis canadensis*, is another tree of ill-repute, although in this case, except in its form *C. siliquastrum 'Alba'*, it lacks the requirement of white flowers. Reddish-purple seedpods are, however, present. On this ominous tree Judas is said to have died by his own hand, and even those lacking religious feeling are reluctant to cut it, especially during flowering or after dark. In 1937 the Oklahoma Legislature made the redbud the state's official tree: at once a flood of indignant telegrams began to reach Governor Marland, while public meetings of protest were led by the General Federation of Women's Clubs: complaints continued well into the 1940s and the disquiet is still not quite forgotten.

In England the elder, never struck by lightning, it is said, and saving both house and garden from sorcery, is perhaps the most widely regarded tree of reputation. The weather never changes when the delicate-petalled milk-white elder flowers are in bloom (in view of the variability of English summer weather, a considerable tribute to the power of the White Goddess). Germans tip their hats to elder; and gipsies call it *yakori bengeskro*—'devil's eye'—because of its gleaming black berries which, gathered on Midsummer Eve, protect their possessor from witchcraft. (Berries from the red elder are equally valuable.) In the Christian tradition the elder is yet another tree upon which Judas hanged himself and, since it provided wood for the cross, if used for firewood it 'raises the devil' (an interesting blend of pagan and Christian mythology). To fell or prune an elder, especially after nightfall, angers the Hyldemör or Elder Mother and the Danes, fearful of offending, used a conciliatory formula if cutting were unavoidable:

> *Lady Elder, give me thy wood,*
> *And I will give thee of mine,*
> *When I become a tree!*

Children have for many generations been warned never to touch the elder's 'poisonous' leaves and berries ('Rank poison,' cried the writer's grandfather when offered a glass of excellent elderberry wine). The leaves, berries, sap and wood, if malodorous, tart and largely valueless, are harmless enough and the adjuration is a shadowy recollection of the tree's earlier preeminence: it was wiser to train children to leave such a tree severely alone.

Jack Morley, gardener at Kennel Moor, Godalming, states that in West Surrey country people believe elder wood and bark to be physically warmer than that of other trees, because in southern England, at least, elder blooms around Midsummer Day, the peak of the sun's yearly strength. At midsummer the umbellate elder flowers at their richest and whitest are a fitting aspect of the Goddess; the tree's wood is therefore chosen for the perches and shelves of hen-houses so that laying hens may also benefit from the Goddess's benign fertility magic.[10] Thomas Hyll, the Tudor gardener, recommended elder hedges for gardens and the tradition endures, although more rarely seen than in 1827 when John Clare, the Northamptonshire poet, wrote:

> *The maids hang out white clothes to dry*
> *Around the elder-skirted croft . . .*

and Richard Jefferies said of a north Wiltshire cottage in the latter part of the century:

> The cottage . . . was . . . half thatched, and half slated, with a narrow slip of a flower-garden, full of hollyhocks, sunflowers and wallflowers, enclosed in a high elder-hedge . . .

And a respect for the tree lingers: a Devon correspondent writes:

> A professional gardener friend of mine told me that an elder in your garden is very lucky, especially if self-sown, and should be given a place to grow as it keeps evil influences away[11]

and another from Dorset:

> There is an elder by the old kitchen door of our house and I think that this
> tree was an anti-witch device ... we regularly chop it, but have not re-
> moved it; the old kitchen is now only a workshop, but I wonder some-
> times if our motives are not deeper rooted than the tree ... .[12]

Some authorities, on the other hand, with an eye to the later traditions of the sky-gods, have described certain plants and trees as 'lightning plants': holly, fern, parsley, hawthorn, elder, gooseberry, house-
leek, mistletoe, oak and rowan, they say, all possess at least one of th e
following characteristics: pinnate, pinnatifid or deeply-serrated leaves;
forked growth; scarlet or yellow berries or flowers; or thorns— all
shapes and colours typifying the dancing patterns of lightning. Such
plants sprang therefore from the sacred fire of the sky gods Thor and
Jupiter. By revering the gods' plants, man took on a lease of their
inviolability and saved his household from fire, lightning and witchcraft. Such gods rivalled but never outshone the White Goddess. All
provided their followers with a variety of helpful plants.

Lightning plants retain magical links with enchantment, invisibility,
birth, death and weather. Bishop Heber, travelling near Boitpoor,
Upper India, about 1810, and knowledgeable about magic, found another candidate for the list, apparently the *Mimosa catechu*, the 'sacred
thorn':

> I passed a fine tree of the mimos genus, with leaves, at a little distance, so
> much resembling those of the mountain ash, that I was for a moment de-
> ceived, and asked if it did not bring fruit. They answered no; but that it
> was a very noble tree, being called the imperial tree, for its excellent
> properties; that it was useful as a preservative against magic. A sprig worn
> in the turban, or suspended over the bed was perfect security against all
> spells, evil eye, etc. inasmuch as the most formidable wizard would not, if
> he could help it, approach its shade. One indeed, they said, who was very
> renowned for his power of killing plants and drying up their sap with a
> look, had come to this very tree and gazed on it intently; but, said the old
> man, who told me this with an air of triumph, look as he might, he could
> do the tree no harm. I was amazed and surprised to find the superstition
> which in England and Scotland attaches to the rowan tree here applied to a
> tree of nearly similar form. What nation has in this been the imitator? Or
> from what common centre are these common notions derived?[13]

Holly's good name as much as its handsome appearance, accounts for the hundreds of 'Holly Cottages' in the English countryside. Its prickly leaves and berries of burning coral-red, fulfilling all the requirements of magic, are peculiarly abhorrent to witches and, since it is clearly unwise to heedlessly trim such a portentous tree, spreading hollies stand sentinel, scarcely pruned from one generation to the next, in many hedgerows and gardens. A correspondent from Lowestoft writes: 'A holly tree must always be planted near the kitchen door to "keep evil spirits away"—I planted one myself';[14] echoing Pliny's *'Aquifolia arbor, in domo aut villâ sata, veneficia arcet'*—'Holly trees round the house prevent sorcery.' In another striking example of how widespread are the most antique plant beliefs, a Japanese gardener, Yoshimasa Ishii of Tokyo, said in 1976 that in his garden, where plants are chosen for their aesthetic and symbolic value, a holly tree stands guardian by the front door 'to scatter evil spirits'. Holly hedges, now well-grown, and still surrounding certain Cambridgeshire cottages, are said to have been planted as barriers by superstitious Scottish prisoners, skilled in protective magic, brought south after the battle of Dunbar in 1650 to assist in draining the Fens. No beast injures magical holly and a tree self-sown ('growing volunteer' as American gardeners say) is of special virtue:

> A friend of mine was told by an old gardener that if a holly sows itself in your garden it should never be disturbed: it will bring good luck to the owner of the garden. As two—self-sown—have established themselves in my garden, I shall, needless to say, let them remain![15]

The word 'rowan' is derived from the Swedish *rön* and is connected with 'rune': rowan could be properly translated as 'magic tree'. In the 'highland zone', that is northern England, Wales and Scotland, the rowan is the cardinal keeper of the cottage door: its berries, like those of holly, honeysuckle and red elders, are inimical to witchcraft. Scarlet is the most telling anti-witch colour of all. In Newfoundland rowan sprigs were set down the rows of crops as protection. About 1860 the Rev George Ormsby felled a rowan in his carriage drive and encountered a prejudice: 'The old man who gardens for me came a day or two after and was strangely disconcerted on seeing "what master had done in his absence" for, said he, "Wherever a wiggan-tree grows near a house the witches canna come." He was, however, greatly comforted by the discovery of a rowan sucker which had been overlooked during the destruction.'[16]

The wood of the ash, *Fraxinus excelsior*—the 'husbandman's tree'—is renowned for tool handles and walking sticks; formerly at least this use was derived from the great dislike witches have for ash-wood, as well as from the natural excellence of the wood for the purpose. An iron tool with ashwood handle promised security indeed for its owner. Despite modern technology the practical aspect of the tradition survives and Spear and Jackson, among other garden tool makers, advertise specifically that their tools have 'wax-finished ash shafts'. Garden tools have lore of their own. From Alabama to Dorset a spade must never be carried indoors:

> *For if in your house a man shoulders a spade,*
> *For you and your kinsfolk a grave is half made.*

Any sharp tool, such as a hoe, accidentally brought into the house, must be at once removed by the same way, or it will 'cut' the household's good fortune. To lay a rake on the ground teeth uppermost causes ill-luck, a poor crop, or rain. To correct the latter effect the gardener if female—must curtsey to the sun in apology as she picks up her tool. Negroes of the American South say that a gardener who leaves a hoe upright in the garden after the day's work will lie sleepless that night.[17]

Red-fruited mulberry and yellow quince trees must be planted in partnership. A visitor to a Warwickshire garden about 1905, shown a flourishing mulberry, disconcerted his host with the question 'Where's the quince? Don't you know that a quince must always be planted near a mulberry or ill-luck will cling to the house?' A search was hastily made: a few yards away in the underbrush a quince was found—'The situation was saved!' The mulberry should stand on the south side of the house and the quince, fruit of love which, according to Pliny, keeps the evil eye from the house, on the north: only *its* presence offsets the unfortunate influences of the mulberry, whose fruit was stained red by the blood of the ill-starred lovers, Pyramus and Thisbe. The Japanese, however, add the mulberry to the 'lightning plants' and, since a mulberry is never struck by lightning, repeat the word *kuwabara*

—'mulberry grove'—during storms, to deceive the thunder-god and deflect the stroke.

Ivy too is a guardian, and its withering on the house-wall portends domestic disaster. Sweetbriar, with its scent of spice and apples, and honeysuckle over the door keep both witches and fever at bay. Lilac has virtue: nearly every old American house has its lilac in the yard and Great-Great-Grandmother Blackmer was remembered by her Vermont family as having in 1801 planted purple lilacs at the diagonals of her daughter's house at Rupert to guard it against evil spirits. The hollyhock and family are also valuable: French gardeners favoured hedges of tree-mallow, of the *Malvaceae*. According to a German legend a dwarf abducted a peasant woman, to whom he said as they passed through the flowering garden:

> *Heb auf dein Gewand*
> *Dass du nicht fallest im Dosten und Dorant*

—'Lift up your hem, so that you may not fall among the origanum and snapdragons.' His quick-witted victim immediately stepped on these safeguarding plants and escaped: snapdragons break charms. A protective box or juniper bush growing at the doorstep halts a witch who must pause and count every leaf before working woe.[18] In the ancient world the richly-red peony was said to glow at night and to keep evil spirits from the garden. Whether the glow was metaphysical or natural was not clear; but today a plant novelty is the lemon-peel-scented 'gas plant', *Dictamnus fraxinella*, whose volatile vapour on sultry evenings flashes and burns when lighted with a match.

The supernatural reputation of many plants clearly originated in the pagan world: Christianity also contributed. Rosemary, a powerful disperser of evil, whose flowers turned blue when the Virgin Mary threw her cloak over them, gained sanctity from the encounter. William Brown, who lives in a fifteenth-century cottage by the churchyard at Stockleigh Pomeroy, Devon, and who can touch a tombstone as he leans from his window, writes: 'To keep ghosts out I grow rosemary and other "spirit stoppers"!'[19] The stately white madonna lily, *Lilium candidum*, so splendid in cottage gardens, also keeps ghosts from the house with its holy aura, and will only grow for a *good* woman. Mrs E. V. Longman of Ferndown, Dorset, tells of another tradition:

> Our elderly next-door neighbour had a wonderful clump of Christmas roses in her garden. She gave us a portion of the plant, and we have at times bought new plants, but they never grew. I asked the neighbour one day why she was so lucky and we were not. She said 'Well, my dear, you must always plant a Christmas Rose near your front door to welcome Christ into your house!' . . . I have tried three new plants in the garden of this cottage. Two I planted where we wanted them and they died: the third we planted by our front door, where it is blooming nicely.[20]

IRON AND SALT: STONES AND BONES

Iron has a high protective reputation which has remained undimmed for thousands of years. At least some of the modern partiality for wrought iron gates and decorative garden ironwork flows from this primeval respect for the metal: compared with wood—and today plastics—iron is awkward to work and hard to maintain; its popularity must therefore be justified on other grounds.

How did iron, not to modern eyes an exotic substance, gain such enduring character? It is possible that when this seemingly-magical metal was first used by man for tools and weapons some thousands of years ago its rarity and the mystery of its working, with its notable advantages over the previously worked stone, bronze and horn, invested it with supernatural powers. 'Cold iron' was a daunting substance to friend and foe alike: it spelt martial superiority, economic strength and psychic safety, and iron's effectiveness against human enemies was so marked that it was natural for it to seem protective against occult foes also. The earliest iron worked by man was meteoric, thrown down in anger by Thor, ruler of thunder and thunderbolts, and this dramatic source gave added weight to the charm. Iron has many uses. An iron poker laid across the hearth keeps 'Old Lob' away; those restoring old houses may find groups of iron nails driven into walls, apparently purposelessly but intended as a protective zareba to halt a witch's progress through the house. Decorative iron boot-scrapers at the house-door are as protective as they are practical.

Any object presenting two forks or horns—including, of course, the moon herself—is said to possess occult power and this, with the iron from which they were made, gave special potence to horseshoes. It is a virtue still understood. An inspection of allotment huts in a Yorkshire manufacturing town a few years ago revealed that, of thirty-two huts, eleven bore horseshoes over their doors. In Kentucky and among the Pennsylvanian Germans, iron plough points hang from fruit trees to 'draw the frost'. In Fredericksburg, Gillespie County, Texas, with many German settlers, four horseshoes were seen suspended from one fruit tree and a branch had grown right over an ancient shoe resting in a fork. In North Carolina iron 'junk' from round the farm was buried under apple trees to encourage fruiting. Although some gardeners explain that iron salts are beneficial to fruit (and others bury a bag of iron nails beneath a pink hydrangea to turn its flowers blue) there seems little doubt, in view of iron's prophylactic character, that the real intention, for more superstitious gardeners at any event, is to banish sorcery from garden and orchard. 'It would make the fruit hold on', said some: the evil eye expertly causes fruit to fall!

Perhaps it is not all magic. Dr George Starr White, author of *Cosmo-Electric Culture*, reports that metals such as iron and tin, dangling from fruit trees, do promote growth. When Randall Groves Hay, an industrial engineer from Jenkintown, New Jersey, experimented by hanging metallic Christmas tree decorations from fifteen tomato plants, the fruit thus decorated ripened in inclement weather, earlier than usual and long before the crops of other growers.

Pieces of iron have come to light during the felling of old trees. In the heart of a giant elm felled in 1973 in the grounds of Meadows School, Southborough, Kent, was found a 4½-inch iron stake: when the famed Pittsfield elm was felled in Massachusetts in the nineteenth century a crooked iron staple was revealed deep in its wood. These of course could be mere relics of former hitching stakes but their situation makes this unlikely. Elms have proven protective qualities and the shade of an elm, said the Romans, was salubrious and nourishing to any plant growing beneath it: iron probably intensified these powers. The old elm on Parker Street, Old Newbury, also in Massachusetts, is traditionally said to have grown from a slip planted by Richard Jaques in 1713. One evening he stayed late with his sweetheart and emerging into darkness ' . . . plucked him a twig well clothed with leaves' from the elm at the cottage door as a talisman against bewitchment on his homeward journey. This passed safely and he planted the twig which eventually grew into what many regarded as the largest elm in New England.[21]

In West Surrey and Buckinghamshire, ironstone slabs from local quarries made neat black paths for cottages or were worked as protective and decorative 'garnetting' into the mortar of house and garden walls; Gertrude Jekyll, the garden designer, was familiar with this device and, enjoying the tradition, used it herself in garden buildings which included the significantly-named Thunder House, where she and her friends gathered to watch storms blowing up darkly behind the Surrey hills. In Scandinavian mythology Thor, drawn across the rumbling heavens in his goat-drawn wagon, was god of thunderbolt *and* iron, his metal at once his weapon and man's protection against it. Gilbert White of Selborne wrote in the eighteenth century in his Hampshire–Surrey border country, of garnetting so common that 'strangers sometimes ask us pleasantly "whether we fastened our walls together with tenpenny nails" '. The chips of ironstone were the size of a large nail—once sold at tenpence for a hundred.[22]

In West Africa 'crop-irons', crescent-shaped charms upon long spikes set among crops, save them from 'overlooking' by the evil eye. In England long crooked iron braces still support old house and garden walls: two bisecting each other form the conventionalized *Mjolnir* or 'hammer of Thor', the god's weapon, most powerful of all charms against lightning and magic: today such irons are seen as functional only but in the past their protective role was warmly appreciated.

Witches fear salt, prime symbol of incorruptibility. No witch (let alone Satan himself) will step over salt. Lawrence Eochard of Christ's College, Cambridge, a traveller in Ireland in 1690, wrote that there 'before sowing the corn some salt is flung on the earth': a gesture which Lady Wilde was to find still common in 1890. Apparently this magico-manurial practice still finds favour with Irishmen. C. E. Terry, secretary of the Osmaston Park Allotments Association in Derby, wrote in 1974: 'We had a southern Irish member who used about one hundredweight of salt each season, until my committee (perhaps fearing damage to the soil) condemned the practice and terminated his tenancy.' He may well have been recalling the old superstition—but in fairness it must be admitted that the tenant who followed him enjoyed wonderful crops of cabbages and broad beans![23]

The pockets of many gardeners hold a 'lucky-stone' or fossil, found during digging. A fossil sea-urchin, its neat cone inscribed with ray-like fine lines, has been a sun—and therefore a prosperity—symbol since the Bronze Age. Sea-urchins had magical uses and were often included in burials where their magic would warm the dead. One Bronze Age man buried on Dunstable Downs was surrounded by scores of sea-urchins. Later their loaf shape (another folk name is 'fairy-loaf') linked them with the family's food supply: a sea-urchin fossil might stand on the mantelpiece of an East Anglian cottage to ensure, through the magic of analogy, bread for the household. It was a no less potent stimulant for garden crops.

The slender, spiked bullet-like belemnite, commonest of fossils, is valued as a protective amulet from Europe to Australia: in Germany as *teufelsfinger*, 'devil's finger', or *donnerstein*, 'thunderstone'; in the French Alps as *pierre de tonnerre*. Red Indians believe that a 'thunderbolt' or belemnite is formed whenever lightning strikes the ground: in Suffolk thunderstones 'fell from shooting stars or during storms'. In fact, the fossil is the guardbone of an extinct form of cuttlefish.

There is much confusion over the word thunderstone, which may apply to the belemnite, to a prehistoric flint or stone implement, to iron pyrites or to a meteorite. Any of these objects turned up during digging is worth the gardener's attention. The Pitt Rivers Museum in Oxford shows a cluster of iron pyrites found in Canton Graubunden, Switzerland, during potato digging by peasants who kept it in the house as a protection against storms.

Many fossils are luck-bringers. Names are picturesque. In Yorkshire saurian fossils are 'fallen angels' bones'; elephants' teeth are 'giants' teeth'; nummulites 'penny shells' or 'Pharaoh's beads'; the vertebrae of ichthyosaurs or plesiosaurs 'salt-cellars'; the chalk coral of Kent 'brains'; and encrinites St 'Cuthbert's beads', 'fairy millstones' or 'wheelstones'. Still agreeable for the gardener is the find of the whitish, glassy pebble called a 'godstone', cherished where found from northern England to Hertfordshire. One Lancashire gardener sent the writer a godstone in 1974 and advised that it be thrown over the right shoulder, for luck.[24]

Above left, peas, which should be planted at the moon's waxing. *Above right*, plums, a magical colouring aid for peaches. *Below left*, broad beans grow 'backwards in the pod' in leap years. *Below right*, protective rowan.

Above, quince (*left*) and mulberry (*right*) trees should be grown near each other for good luck. *Below left*, sage, an index to domestic ascendancy. *Below right*, a box bush at the doorstep effectively prevents a witch from entering.

From ancient times, naturally-holed 'hag-stones' have hung in house and stable against witchcraft. The hagstone represents the All-Seeing Eye of ancient mythology, a world-wide apotropaic device intended 'to look back at' and thus deflect the envious powers of the evil eye, and it appears in many contexts from the prows of Mediterranean fishing-boats to the front boards of East Anglian farm wagons. When the writer noticed a holed beach stone tied to the key of a garden shed at Hastings, Sussex, the elderly owner would say only: 'You leave it alone. I always have a lucky-stone for my key. Things won't go right otherwise.' Hagstones (found too in the thatch of old houses or hanging from nails in the cowshed) were seen in a cottage garden at Frogham, Hampshire, in the nineteen-fifties as a massive necklace dangling protectively between two ancient apple trees.[25]

In his *Narrative of a Mission to Central Africa* (1853) Richardson wrote:

> To avert the evil eye from the gardens, the people (or Mourzak) put up the head of an ass, or some portion of the bones of that animal. The same superstition prevails in all the countries that stud the North of Africa, from Egypt to the Atlantic, but the people are unwilling to explain what special virtue there exists in an ass's skull.

English tastes of the fifteenth to eighteenth centuries perhaps had similar roots. When, about 1750, Peter Kalm, the Swedish traveller, called on Peter Collinson at Peckham, England, he found the garden beds bordered with the knuckle bones of horses and oxen 'rounded, curled ends uppermost', and remembered seeing similar bones decorating gardens round Moscow.

Bones are protective devices of antiquity, once as foundation sacrifices to make buildings stand more surely. At first such sacrifices were human but by the Middle Ages animal bones were acceptable substitute magic. Finds of bones in walls and thatch of old buildings are not uncommon and their use seems to have been widely sanctioned until at least the eighteenth century when, under the duress of the Age of Reason, such superstitions went into decline. But when the idea of sacrifice in the central buildings of the homestead was no longer acceptable, it is interesting to find that bones continued to be used widely in garden buildings, walls and follies.

It could of course be argued that bones were chosen because of a shortage of decorative materials; but the facts do not bear this out.

H

England, particularly, is rich in beach pebbles, stone quarries and fossils. Ted Humphris wrote that the floor in the circular summerhouse at Aynho was of pebbles selected from gravel pits on the estate (pointing to a very convenient supply of pleasing materials) and of *knucklebones* of deer killed in Aynho Park. At Kedleston, the Derbyshire home of Viscount Scarsdale, the Bone House, decorated with large oxtail bones, was built for Lady Curzon about 1740. At Goodwood House, Sussex, is the Shell Grotto built in the seventeen-forties by the second Duchess of Richmond and her daughters *with their own hands*; its mosaic walls are of coloured shells, its floor of marble decorated with horses' teeth. The thatched Bear's Hut, at Killerton, Devon, which once housed a pet bear brought home by a soldier grandson of the Acland family, is another example, with a floor of knucklebones of sheep and deer.[26] Many garden houses were decorated by the ladies of the household: it was a favourite feminine pastime until into the nineteenth century. But on consideration it seems most improbable that fastidious women of taste and sensitivity would have willingly handled sacks of unpleasant slaughterhouse materials unless there were a compelling, if unrevealed, inner reason for doing so. It was more than a fashion: people only do what is needful to them. Perhaps it is not too outlandish to hypothesize that a liking for this particular magic lingered, and that when bone sacrifices were no longer appropriate for the house it was still felt a wise insurance to continue to use them for lesser buildings on the property, just as the protective horseshoe gradually moved from the front door of the house to the door of the kitchen, stable or garden shed.

Bucrania, ox-skulls in plaster, often appear as a decoration in classical summerhouses. The circular chamber of the Pantheon at Stourhead, Wiltshire, for example, is decorated with a frieze of skulls and garlands. In ancient times skulls were nailed to the extremities of tie-beams of timber buildings, which projected beyond the supporting walls into the weather. As well as protecting the exposed timbers, skulls also saved the occupants of the building from lightning and witchcraft: like the hagstone the uncompromising glare of the eye sockets of a skull was a valuable antidote to the ill-intentioned glance. When stone tended to replace timber in buildings, corbels decorated with stone representations of the heads of men and beasts took the place of real skulls: in time these were replaced or augmented with stone balls, urns or pine-apples, still common as decorative finials for gateposts, summerhouses and garden walls, recalling primitive magic.

THE SIGN OF THE CROSS

Crops marked with a cross-sign by hand or by sticks can never be over-looked by those with the evil eye, or by fairies. In the Celtic tradition which makes perilous the junctions between time periods, fairy raids take place on the last night of every quarter, especially before 1 May (*Beltane*) or 1 November (*Samhain*). 'Watch closely on May Eve and May Day for anything unusual among your plants: the witches set their spells then,' writes Mrs Hayes from Dublin.[27]

Combining pagan trees with Christian symbols, gardeners happily invoked protective magic emanating from entirely contrary sources. In Herefordshire on May morning seedbeds were spiked with small pro-tective crosses of rowan and birch: a Chepstow woman said, 'My father used also to put some hawthorn twigs in each seedbed to make null and void the witches' spells.' In Ireland special attention was paid to the muckheap as the source of fertility for farm and garden alike, and in the Glens of Antrim a green sprig was stuck protectively upon it on May Eve when the fairies would essay their greatest mischief.[28]

In Ireland great reliance is placed on the hazel tree as a counter to witchcraft. A gardener who with a hazel stick draws a circle round himself and his garden ensures that no witch, fairy or evil spirit can enter; but to be effective the stick must have been cut on May morning, before sunrise. Ruth Tongue remembers helping an old Somerset cottager in his garden and at his request making the charm sign, a heart between crosses, with a hazel stick on the newly-turned earth of the spring seedbed. She has seen this sign once or twice thereafter, tucked away discreetly in a secret corner of a cottage garden, against the depradations of 'vairies'. In similar fashion European peasants ploughed a cross into each corner of a field in spring: the making of the cross concluded planting.

To ancient peoples trees were phallic symbols: sacred groves were common to many cults. This symbolism was to become confused with the 'cross-tree' of Christianity. In monastery orchards in the Middle

Ages apple trees were piously planted in cruciform rows and the whole form of an apple-tree mystically linked with the cross, the trunk to the shaft, the branches to the transverse members. Apple-wood was another from which the cross was said to have been made. The apple-tree's strongly holy and magical reputation in the pre-Christian period should be remembered—and its place in Greek, Roman and Norse myths. The apple grew in the Celtic paradise where hills were clothed with trees bearing fruit and blossom together: today the ominous importance of this occurrence (described in the following chapter) could well be a distorted memory of this Celtic myth. The destruction of an orchard was almost sacrilegious and no garden planted in an orchard's stead could be expected to thrive.

There are other cruciform beliefs: since all members of the *Cruciferae* (including cabbage, wallflower, stock and alyssum) bear flowers with four petals arranged cross-wise, old herbalists declared that no member of the family could be poisonous. There were further cultural procedures. *A Short Introduction Very Profitable and Necessary for All Those that Delight in Gardening* (1592) said explicitly: 'Coleworts [cabbages such as sea kale and rape] white and greene must be sowen in February or March in an old moon and in such a sygne X it is good to replant them.'

'My father always slashed an X upon a cabbage stump to "encourage the growth of greens",' writes Mrs A. F. Smith of Patchway, Bristol, describing a widely known rationalization of an old protective device to secure the cabbage patch against the plant demon.[29] There could perhaps be a further intention: German woodmen once made the sign of the cross upon the stump of a newly felled tree to enable the tree's spirit to continue to live in the stump. A little different in concept is the custom noted among the islanders of remote Pitcairn who mark every tenth row of their crops with a cross and call it 'God's row': since about 1850 the Pitcairners have been Seventh Day Adventists, a sect which continues, in old style, to give a tithe of produce to the church.

A traveller on the road from Padua to Florence in the last century noticed another cross-form in the vineyards, where trees supporting the vines had been trained laboriously into a curious and elaborate form, suggesting the trident of Siva, from which developed the *trushul* or cross of the gipsies. This shape was certainly not the easiest to have achieved and it was certainly not essential to successful viticulture, but the vineyard workers, otherwise taciturn, affirmed with Delphic brevity that 'it brought good luck'.[30]

THE DEVIL'S OFFERING

The notion of leaving a small corner of farm or garden uncultivated as a *douceur* to malignant forces is a surviving device. In 1973 a Buckinghamshire gardener was heard to reprove his assistant, about to weed and tidy the last corner of the garden: 'Leave it be. We musn't be too tidy.' It was left untended. In New England this is 'leaving a tithe to nature'; Ulstermen speak of the 'devil's half-acre' or the 'lone acre', a piece of land left in undisputed control of a higher authority; Welshmen make 'the devil's offering'; Scots preserve the 'gudeman's field' or 'Cloutie's croft'; in England it was 'Jack's land'; and in Nigeria 'the bad bush'. Rarely was the beneficiary of the land directly named. An old man in Cork recently transferred these precautions into garden dimensions when he said of his potato patch 'we must always leave one little bit of a ridge for the "frost": sure it must have something to eat.' The earliest recipient of this particular offering must surely have been a powerful weather god.

Danegelds to dark powers were offered at seed-sowing time: they ensured good crops. Suffolk children dibbling seed in the nineteenth century used an expressive rhyme such as:

> *Four seeds in a hole*
> *One for the birds*
> *One for the mice*
> *And one for the* Master.

The farmer?—or a more sinister bystander? In Ashe County, North Carolina, the sower tosses over his shoulder onto the prepared seedbed a token offering of seed he is to plant, accompanied by the very plain incantation:

> *This is for* me
> *This is for my* neighbour
> *This is for the* Devil.

Another widespread conciliatory practice, still familiar to many gardeners, if today only as a joke, is to leave, by design or accident, small apples on the trees for the 'birds' or 'fairies' at the end of apple harvest. Generally children were allowed to steal them in the allusively-named sport of 'pisking', 'griggling' or 'pixy-hoarding'. In Cornwall it was felt to be most unlucky to return to search for apples overlooked at the main picking—the owner's departure from his orchard should leave it free for other visitors—and in Holstein, Germany, five or six apples were always left upon each tree 'to ensure a proper crop in the following year'.

5

PLANTS, PERSONALITIES
AND PREDICTIONS

Recent research has brought age-old beliefs bearing on the personality of plants and their links with human life into fresh prominence. Confirmed by eye-witnesses from earliest times, life-indexes, communication between plant and plant and plant and owner, and the ability of plants to reveal events—these and other responses are now being investigated.

GREEN FINGERS AND THUMBS

American gardeners possessing the enviable knack of making plants grow have 'green thumbs', Britons 'green fingers': both countries speak of the 'brown', 'black' or 'purple' fingers of those less favourably endowed. 'My grandfather,' said a correspondent in *Bygones* in 1883, 'would never engage a labourer on his farm without first ascertaining if hedges would grow after his cutting them,' for along the Welsh border it was said that the very touch of some workers was so destructive that hedges planted or pleached by them would never thrive again. In North Carolina old people preternaturally successful at turnip sowing are believed to possess some secret touch or incantation,[1] and the Maryland plantations all boasted their green-thumbed 'lucky' or 'planting hand'—a worker with greater abilities than average to make seed germinate who would be detailed to plant a row or two to start the work on a satisfactory basis before everyone joined in.[2] The ability —or inability—to make plants thrive has been recognized by many: Beverley Nichols, an expert gardener, speaks of his own inexplicable failure with certain plants, despite the best attention, and attributes this to some spell cast unwittingly. Why, otherwise, did *Tropaeolum speciosum*, the climbing flame nasturtium, refuse to grow with him— although other gardeners reported successes with it in the most ill-favoured backyards?[3] ('Grows like weeds!' trumpeted an advertiser in *Exchange and Mart* in 1905.)

Green fingers are no respecters of persons. In New Delhi, India, in 1975, Prince Charles, shown trees which his mother Queen Elizabeth II of England and his father Prince Philip had planted during earlier visits, observed that the queen's tree, although younger, was the taller: 'The trees that my mother plants always grow well but not those planted by my father.'

Many have contemplated the mysteries of this gift. Russell Page in *The Education of a Gardener* (1962) calls green fingers 'the extension of a verdant heart' and believes that good gardens can be made only by gardeners who understand plants in a very real sense. Luther Burbank, the American plant breeder, believed that love was a vital source of nourishment essential to plant raising. Burbank assured his plants of his appreciation of them and asked for their help in producing new strains; and his relationship with nature and with plants was so legendary that, during the San Francisco earthquake of 1906, it was remarked that although much of the city was destroyed not a single pane of glass in Burbank's greenhouses was broken, nor a single plant injured.[4]

PLANT TO PLANT: PLANT TO OWNER

Metaphysical links between one plant and another have long been conjectured. The much respected scientist Sir Humphry Davy, inventor of the miner's lamp, held that transplanted shoots of a tree would live only so long as the parent tree and that, when the parent died, so would the child, even if they were miles apart. It was a matter of contagious magic: a relationship between part and whole, once forged, endures forever.

On his Pennsylvanian farm J. I. Rodale, the American organic gardening authority, planted slips from two coleus plants, then destroyed one parent by burning and buried its remains far away. Although they did not die, slips from the burned plant grew markedly less well than those from the surviving parent. It must be conceded, of course, that the gardener's personality and his guilty knowledge of his destructive act could well be powerful inhibitors in such experiments. Gardeners in Louisiana say that to destroy one plant in the garden causes all others there of the same species to die: lilacs and laburnums particularly resent the felling of one of their number and in protest fail to bloom during the following season.

A tree always does best near a 'friend':

> A few years ago I was given a golden holly from the garden at Great Dixter, Sussex, but for three years it made little progress here. I then remembered that Mr Cyril Litten, the Parks Superintendent at Caterham, once told us that plants preferred to be with their own kind, so I replanted the golden holly by a common green holly, and it is now doing excellently,

records Mrs M. C. Baker from Weston Turville, Buckinghamshire. 'If you take plants when you remove to a new home be sure to plant them near to each other. They will be happier near old friends,' writes another correspondent.[5]

Empathy between plant and owner is strong. Mrs Longman writes from Ferndown, Dorset:

> When we moved to the town house, we bought a young willow tree which grew in the front garden to be sturdy and picturesque. After about eight years we sold the house and left the neighbourhood. I chanced one day to meet the new owner and he asked me whether we had 'fed' the tree with anything special for it was now dying, and he felt it was pining for us. I had heard that one must talk to willows or they became lonely, so I returned to the house and talked to the tree and asked it what was wrong. After this it revived and continued to improve. Unfortunately we were then unable to see it again for some time, and when we finally made the visit the poor tree had died and had been removed. Since then I have heard stories of other willows actually pining for people. My friend looked after her sister's garden during her holiday and within two weeks a willow there was dead. Neighbours of another friend put their bungalow up for sale and left the district: they asked my friend to keep an eye on the garden until the new owner took over. Just as mysteriously that willow, too, died.[6]

Mrs Pearl Unger of the Borough of Queens, New York, describes the effect of her illness upon her plants. Mrs Unger entered hospital for an operation, taking with her two favourite houseplants, a *Maranta* and an *Oxalis Regnellii*, both blooming; but when she returned from the operating theatre she found that the plants had collapsed.[7] The sceptical would of course suggest that unfamiliar air conditioning or the unsympathetic hand of a nurse caused this dramatic prostration: separating speculation from fact is a major difficulty in arriving at the truths of plant sensitivity, but the understanding between plants and owners revealed by research suggests that in this case at least the collapse could well have been sympathetic rather than coincidental.

LIFE AND DEATH

Links between owners and trees—'life-indexes'—may be forged early and formally. In the nineteenth century in Canton Aargau, Switzerland, an apple tree was planted for the birth of a boy, a pear for a girl, and the child would flourish or languish with the tree.[8] Hebrews favoured cedars for boys and pines for girls. The idea is regaining popularity in England and, on 17 January 1976, *Amateur Gardening* published a photograph of four-year-old Mark Hopking of Castle Hedingham, Essex, looking at his 'birth tree', a *Metasequoia glyptostroboides* which, as a two-year-old tree, was planted when Mark was two, to keep the ages of tree and child in unison.

Sophisticated and simple alike have felt the charm of life-indexes. When Lord Byron first visited his ancestral home of Newstead Abbey, Nottinghamshire, 'he planted ... a young oak in some part of the grounds, and had an idea that, as *it* flourished, so should *he*'.[9] Planting a tree is almost like life insurance, and the owner can expect to absorb the tree's sturdy vitality and longevity into his own life pattern. The emperors of the Manchu dynasty of China took the air in a tiny private garden in the forbidden city of Peking where all the trees were clipped into formal shapes, except for one, 'the life tree of the dynasty', which was allowed to sprawl unchecked for upon its abundant growth depended the wellbeing and continuance of the royal house.

Numberless trees seem prophetically attuned to coming events. When at Porch House, Eardisland, Herefordshire, about 1850, an apparently sturdy walnut tree fell during the night, lugubrious villagers anticipated ill-luck. They had not long to wait. Shortly afterwards the mistress of the house, seemingly as healthy as the tree had been, dropped dead without warning. At Cuckfield Place, Sussex, a limetree in the avenue warns the owner of his imminent death by dramatically depositing a branch across his path. One of the best authenticated life-index stories attaches to the Kempenfelt family. Admiral Richard Kempenfelt and his brother, Gustavus Adolphus, both planted commemorative thorn trees at their home, Lady Place, Berkshire. Later, when the admiral was away with the fleet, Gustavus noticed that Richard's thorn had withered suddenly and died. He expressed fears for his brother's safety and that evening, 29 August 1782, came the news of the disastrous sinking during careening at Spithead of the admiral's flagship the *Royal George*, with the loss of 'twice four hundred men'.

A nineteenth-century treasure of the Hohenzollern Museum, Berlin, was a splinter of wood from an aged pear tree which grew at the foot of the Unsterburg. The tree, it was said, 'would bloom only so long as the German empire flourished'. When in 1806 the empire was dissolved and the Confederation of the Rhine formed, the pear withered and stood apparently lifeless for sixty years until, in 1871, when the new German empire was established, it sprouted, blossomed and fruited once again.[10]

Life-indexes remain much in mind: a correspondent in the *Sunday Express* for 13 January 1974 recalled a World War II experience when his household at Bognor Regis, Sussex, was in the habit of entertaining American servicemen on leave, among them a young pilot from Miami, whose particular favourite among the houseplants was a palmetto in the conservatory, where the visitor spent many hours. The young man returned to duty. Suddenly and inexplicably the palmetto withered and died. Shortly afterwards a letter was received from the squadron chaplain to say that the airman's plane had been lost in action over the North Sea.

Mrs Mary Myers describes another practice akin to life-indexes. As soon as a young child can walk it should be carried into the garden and set down: the first plant that it touches will reveal the character of its future life. There are many possibilities: if, for example, the plant touched is rue, the child may look forward to a life of sorrow; if rosemary, of happiness; lily of the valley, a life of humility and purity; thyme, a single life; and sage, a life of wisdom. All these predictions are based on the ancient reputations and infective magic of garden plants.

TELLING THE PLANTS

Until quite recent years 'telling the bees' of deaths and family happenings was regarded as essential by many country households (indeed the practice is probably not quite obsolete); if this ritual were neglected it was said that the bees might fly away or die. It was no less important to dress houseplants in mourning when a death occurred, lest they too languish in imitation of the deceased.

When, about 1860, the landlady of the First and Last Inn at Land's End, Cornwall, died, the bird cages and flowerpots on the inn windowsills were trimmed for the funeral with black crape bows. The custom was common particularly in the West of England and, in *Walks About St. Hilary* (1838), Mrs Pascoe wrote:

> I saw with my own eyes a little black flag attached to our churchwoman's bit of mignonette, which she assured me had begun to quail since her poor grandson was burnt to death, but which had revived after she had put on it the piece of mourning.

Her daughter in Penzance had had twenty-two flourishing houseplants, she said, which had faded at the time of the accident but quickly revived after enactment of the crape ritual. The plants' participation in the healing ritual of mourning neutralizes the menace of death.

American negroes and European orchardists believe in informing each fruit tree in the orchard of a family death: in Morocco death is formally announced to the tree, which will show its grief and sensitivity by dropping a few leaves, or, in extreme cases, if the deceased himself planted it, by withering right away. In a North Carolinan variant all the seed-pods to be found in the garden at the time of the death must be shaken or their seed will not germinate,[11] and in Germany every flower pot in the funeral house is turned about out of respect for the dead.[12]

'FLOWERS OUT OF SEASON . . .'

Out of season blooming, a sinister interruption of the orderly rhythm of nature, betokens a death or disaster in the family:

Flowers out of season
Trouble without reason.

Particularly dreaded is a second blooming of kniphofia (the red-hot-poker plant), white roses, violets or the snowball tree. But most alarming of all is a second, autumnal, blooming of a fruit tree, especially if fruit and blossom should appear on the tree together:

A bloom on the tree when the apples are ripe,
Is a sure termination of somebody's life

is the gloomy conclusion. A resident of Tenby, Wales, told of a thought-provoking experience about 1850:

Last year I was walking in the garden of a neighbouring farmer, aged seventy-one. We came up to an apple-tree, heavily laden with nearly ripe fruit, and perceived a sprig of very late bloom, a kind of second edition. He told me rather gravely, that in his boyhood this occurrence was invariably held to herald a death in the family in two or three months' time. On my joking him about Welsh credulity, he pretended *not* to believe the idle lore, but was evidently glad to pass from the subject. His brother, aged sixty-eight, in perfect health then, who resided in the same house, was dead within six weeks! A few weeks afterwards walking in our own orchard, I discovered a still later blossom on a Ribstone Pippin tree, and called a man-servant, aged sixty-three, to look at it. He at once told me, with some concern, that it always foretold death in the family; he had known many instances. Singularly enough, he himself was dead in a very few weeks.[13]

In Iowa the second blooming of a cherry was regarded as alarming; in Huntingdonshire it was the pear. In fact, the phenomenon is far from unusual and one Lincolnshire gardener wrote, consolingly: 'There is one apple tree at Bottesford Moor in this parish, on which I have seen one or two late flowers for the last thirty years.'

'MOI, JE PARLE AUX POMMIERS . . .'

Thousands of gardeners enjoy talking to their plants. Fred Streeter, legendary head gardener at Petworth House, Sussex, said in 1974 at the age of 97: 'I give them a bit of encouragement and I get them beaming at me . . . a loving heart's better than green fingers, and sound's more sensible than silence.'[14] And Mrs Goudman of Cardiff, speaking for many gardeners, told the writer: 'I am not an eccentric person but I believe in talking to my pot flowers.'

Flowers rather than vegetables seem to inspire conversations: C. E.
Terry of Osmaston Allotments Association, Derby, writes: 'I have at
least two members who honestly believe in talking to their plants,
particularly greenhouse subjects.' And of William Haycock, in the
unsentimental municipal branch of gardening at Birmingham, Mr
Millington writes: 'I was informed by several of the other gardeners
that Mr Haycock had been seen to talk to plants.' Mrs Hayes adds:
'Plants are living things and thrive on praising.'[15]

In *Garden News* in January 1976 it was revealed that Terry Scott, the
British star of the *Carry On* films and the television series *Hugh and I*,
has similar beliefs. He is quite certain that plants respond to kindness
and hate to feel neglected. When he returns from a theatrical engage-
ment Terry Scott's first action is to walk through his garden en-
couraging the ailing, and thanking those plants that are giving a particularly good display. Rolf Harris, the Australian cabaret singer, is
another believer; in his garden in suburban Kent he talks to his plants
'like the friends they are'. In 1974 during excavations for a swimming
pool in the Harris garden an Australian gum tree became unwell and
seemed about to die: every day Rolf Harris caressed its trunk and
urged it to recover because its beauty would be missed. The patient
responded immediately!

Even professional fruit-growers find time for a chat. Pierre Philion, a
pommologiste in Quebec, says: '*Les femmes parlent aux fleurs. Moi, je
parle aux pommiers.*' M Philion has 3,500 apple trees of his own and
cares for 500,000 more in his job with the provincial government's
department of agriculture. He talks to them all.

Conversations are brisk as often as sentimental: Maggie Baylis of
San Francisco, author of *House Plants for the Purple Thumb* (1974), falls
back on a forthright 'Grow! Damn you!'—much as Guernsey gardeners believed that any herb grew the better for a stimulating curse at
planting time. In the Buckinghamshire village of Stone, Aubrey Woodward talks to his pumpkins and pats them to encourage growth: when
stationed in South Africa in World War II he collected the Africans'
gourd-growing secrets and in 1974 won the first 'giant pumpkin competition' held at his local pub, the Rose and Crown.

Conversation seems to stimulate plants to quite exceptional efforts.
In midwinter in her north-facing apartment the writer urged a *San-*

sevieria trifasciata to bloom: within three weeks four racemes of greenish-white flowers of compelling fragrance had appeared. This plant is not often seen in bloom and this particular specimen, although fully mature for several years, had not in fact flowered before.

MUSICAL PLANTS

Many gardeners feel their plants responsive to music and song. Mrs E. Cheshire of Littlehampton, Sussex, writes of:

> ... cyclamens which my daughter-in-law gave to my friend and me last December: I had a beautiful lavender flowered plant, she a pink. Her plant has already died (I am writing in April) but mine has a dozen flowers and many buds to come. I have heard that plants enjoy music: perhaps this applies to mine, for in the room with the cyclamen I have a piano which is played every day, a wireless and a record player; and my young grandchild plays a recorder there also.[16]

Marty Sussman, owner of a plant shop in the Côte de Luc Shopping Centre, Montreal, believes that plants particularly appreciate classical or oriental music: 'Sitar music is good.' Early in 1975 Mr Sussman hired a string trio to play in his shop one Saturday afternoon such tunes as *Fiddler on the Roof* and Bach's *Minuet in G* to a lush throng of listening yuccas, Norfolk Island pines, rubber plants, *Dracaenas* and *Monstera deliciosas*. He says that experiments show that plants exposed to music grow larger and faster than those beyond its reach: 'I play music in my store all day.' Mr Sussman took a *Philodendron* to a radio show recently and registered its reactions electronically while an announcer read poems sent in by listeners. The plant showed that its favourite poem was 'Where Do I Come From?':

> *One day as I watered*
> *My new baby palm,*
> *She asked me a question,*
> *'Where do I come from?'*

Music and conversation cannot replace proper plant care, Mr Sussman suggests, but a sick fern, for example, might find classical music therapeutic: 'I'd start off with Beethoven and Haydn and go on from there.' Another Quebec nurseryman, who has worked with plants since he was a boy in Holland, agrees: 'Plants are living tissues and living tissues have feelings. I have 150,000 at my place and I can't go round kissing them all good night, but I don't doubt that what they say about them is true.'[17]

A growing body of scientific data illumines these traditional convictions: experiments include those of Dr T. C. N. Singh, head of the department of botany at Annamalai University, Madras, who investigated legends attributing plant growth to music and to the melodious humming of flies and beetles. He asked a friend, Gouri Kumari, to play his stringed *veena* to a group of *Impatiens Balsamina* plants. After a month of music the plants (with controls) were set out of doors, and given equal amounts of water but no food. All the plants burst into flower on 22 November and grew at the same rate for a week; then in the fifth week of the experiment the balsams which had listened to the *veena* shot ahead and by the end of December had 72 per cent more leaves and were 20 per cent taller than the controls. In 1963 Dr Singh recorded in the magazine of the Bihar Agricultural College at Sabour that he had 'proven beyond any shadow of doubt that harmonic sound waves affect the growth, flowering, fruiting and seed yields of plants'. Dr George Milstein's record of *Music to Grow Plants* is marketed in the United States; he believes that such music—which resembles a sonic hum—causes plant stomata to open more fully and thus receive greater quantities of carbon dioxide and water vapour, active factors in plant growth.

Work on the reaction of plants to music has been done by Dorothy Retallack of Denver, Colorado, and, following her example, in an eight-week experiment, two students played music from two Denver radio stations, one classical, the other 'heavy rock', to summer squash plants. Plants exposed to Beethoven, Brahmns, Schubert and other eighteenth- and nineteenth-century composers grew towards the transistor from which the sounds came—one plant twined itself affectionately round the receiver—but plants recoiled from the rock music and bent away up the sides of their glass container, as though in distress. Other experiments showed that rock music at first caused plants either to grow abnormally tall and to put out exceedingly tiny leaves; or to remain stunted. After two weeks one group of marigolds hearing rock had died; an identical group only six feet away, but listening to classical music, was thriving. Rock-stimulated plants demanded far greater quantities of water than the classical group, and the roots of the 'classical marigolds' were in fact four times longer. Particularly disliked was raucous 'acid rock', but the music of the sitar, and to a lesser extent that of such jazz masters as Ellington, Brubeck and Armstrong, pleased the plants which leaned towards the music and showed abundant growth.

TOUCHING AND PRAYING

A sympathetic hand can restore a stricken plant. Mrs Knight of Weston-super-Mare, Avon, writes:

> Twenty years ago two pot plants, brittle, brown and dead to all appearances, were retrieved by my husband from a site which was to be built on by his employers. He brought them home to me; I repotted them, and watched over them, stroking their leaf segments—mere skeletons! Gradually they responded. I am sure that I *willed* those plants to live. They are beautiful and have rewarded me with flowers many times for successive years.[18]

It should be mentioned—although not of course to belittle Mrs Knight's achievement in any way—that the plants concerned were *Epiphyllum Ackermannii*, famed for their toughness and endurance of poor conditions. It would be illuminating to repeat the experiment with a less tolerant subject.

The Religious Research Foundation of America has investigated some of the traditional beliefs concerning the value of prayer for plants, and has found that prayers for growth produce healthy plants, but, supporting the ancient belief that ill-wishers can injure a plant or tree by glance or word, prayers for non-growth induce wilting. The Rev Franklin Loehr, director of the RRFA and author of *The Power of Prayer on Plants* (1969), believes that if cursing works (as Christ cursed the barren figtree: Mark *ii*. 13:21) so will prayer. For half an hour participants in his experiments prayed both personally and communally over a jug of water. Of two sets of planted seeds of corn, lima beans and sweetpeas, one was given 'prayer water', the other untreated water. The corn receiving treated water sprouted first: by the end of the second week seven seeds had germinated in the treated set; only three in the untreated set. Sweet peas did better when among the prayed-for by a margin of three to one. Eventually Mr Loehr had 150 workers, 700 prayer experiments and 27,000 seedlings in his programme and felt that he had clearly established prayer as a force as beneficial to plants as sunlight, bringing about faster germination, sturdier growth and resistance to insect pests.

Methods used varied: blessings, formal or silent, and invocations to the universal life force, a cosmic consciousness, or God, depending upon conviction, were tried. Gardeners were advised to visualize their plants as they would *like* them to be and to provide a regular fifteen-minute prayer session each day, which, it was said, would produce a clear distinction between prayed-over and other plants.

Prayer for plants is an ancient concept: the Elizabethans favoured a formula such as that given by Leonard Mascall of Plumpton Place, Sussex, in the *Booke of the Art and Manner Howe to Plante and Graffe* (1572):

> And, whensoever ye shall plant or graffe it shall be mete and good for you to saye as foloweth:
> In the name of God the Father, the Sonne and the Holy Ghoste, Amen. Increase and multiply, and replenish the earth; and saye the Lorde's prayer, then say: Lord God heare my prayer, and let this desire of thee be hearde. The holy spirite of God which hath created all things for man and hath given them for our comfort, in thy name O Lorde, we set, plant, and graffe, desiring that by thy mighty power they maye encrease, and multiply upon the earth, in bearing plenty of fruite, and the profite, and comfort of all the faithful people . . .

Marcus Terentius Varro, the Roman agriculturalist (116–27 BC), advised that before garden work is commenced the gods be invoked:

> . . . the gods help those who call upon them . . . I do not mean those urban gods whose images stand around the forum, but those twelve gods who are the special patrons of husbandmen. First then, I invoke Jupiter and Tellus, who, by means of the sky and the earth, embrace all the fruits of agriculture; and hence, as we are told that they are the universal parents, Jupiter is called 'the Father', and Tellus is called 'Mother Earth'. And, second, Sol and Luna, whose courses are watched in all matters of planting and harvesting. Third, Ceres and Liber, because their fruits are most necessary for life . . . Fourth, Robigus and Flora; for when they are propitious the rust will not harm the grain and the trees, and they will not fail to bloom in their season . . . Likewise I beseech Minerva and Venus, of whom the one protects the oliveyard and the other the garden . . . And I

shall not fail to pray also to Lympha and Bonus Eventus, since without moisture all tilling of the ground is parched and barren, and without success and 'good issue' it is not tillage but vexation . . .

Some researchers believe that the 'green thumb' depends upon the gardener's 'positive' thoughts—whether knowingly bestowed or not. Marcel Vogel, a Californian research chemist, picked three elm leaves outside his laboratory and concentrated upon two of them, pointedly ignoring a third. Within a week the neglected leaf was dead and dry; the other two remained fresh and green. A group of seeds warned by a South African surgeon that it was too cold for them to grow did not germinate: an identical unwarned group in a nearby pot grew strongly. Positive emotions can be of real assistance to holiday-making gardeners, says Carolyn Busch, a New York plant store owner: plants need never die in these circumstances: 'If you are away from your plants and really love them, and think about them, they won't go downhill.'

Much of the recent interest in plant sensitivity—which throws new light upon a whole range of age-old folk-beliefs—was aroused by the pioneer work of Cleve Backster, an American expert in polygraphy, or lie detection. On 2 February 1966, Backster lightheartedly attached the leaves of a *Dracaena* in his New York office to a polygraph machine and found that the plant exhibited mild emotional stimulation when watered. Further experiments followed. When Backster threatened to burn a leaf the polygraph tracing leapt dramatically in a fear reaction.

Plants were found to be in touch with their owners, distance playing little part. Whenever Backster, miles away on a lecture tour, projected its picture onto the screen, the original *Dracaena* of the first experiment showed a chart reaction. Plants seemed to experience love, hate, fear and anxiety about such menaces to their wellbeing as dogs and ill-disposed humans.

HELP FROM THE DEVAS

Not all supernaturals of the garden are as maleficent as those described in chapter four. One gardening community at least has found their presence of great benefit and indeed essential to its work in every way.

In November 1962 Peter Caddy, his wife Eileen, and Dorothy MacLean of Guelph, Ontario, began to create their garden in the Findhorn Caravan Park, Morayshire, in the bleak north of Scotland on a site then little better than a rubbish heap. Using organic gardening methods, on ground swept by gales, with only broom bushes, marram grass and sparse fir trees for protection and on soil largely of dust, sand and gravel, the Findhorn Community now grows sixty-five vegetables, twenty-one fruits and forty herbs. Visitors have expressed astonishment at Findhorn crops: a cabbage, normally weighing about four pounds, reached forty-two pounds in weight; a delphinium growing in pure sand reached a height of eight feet, and roses customarily bloom amid snow and ice.

The community's members are convinced that they owe their achievements to supernatural assistants. After deep meditation the Caddys were directed by arcane forces to begin work in these inhospitable surroundings, the last place they themselves would have chosen to make a garden, and received instructions to communicate with the *devas*, the higher architects of plant life who control nature spirits and with whom, it is said, gardeners with green fingers are unconsciously in communication. Mystical exchanges have had strikingly practical results: when neighbouring paths became overgrown with gorse, for example, it was explained to the *devas* that the community's walks were being spoiled. The following year no gorse grew upon the paths.

Conclusions drawn at Findhorn seem to support many folk-beliefs. Plants were found to respond to human personality: bad temper is as injurious to plants as happiness is elating. An out-of-humour gardener's black moods may come again to plague those who eat vegetables planted by him on a bad day. The circle easily becomes vicious and descending; or for happier gardeners, ascending, leading to greater joy and satisfaction. The positive gardener must contribute love, happiness and strength to his garden: these qualities, in partnership with practical attention to the requirements of compost and water and with emanations from soil and cosmos, ensure success.

Matthew Shield, head gardener at Findhorn, advised in 1974 that gardeners should chat to their plants casually, as they might to dogs. Flowers never resent picking, say Findhorn gardeners, if the necessity is explained to them; lawns do not object to mowing if their permission is obtained beforehand; pruning, done only when unavoidable, should be discussed first with the tree. Shield believes that every garden however small should have a small wild area where the nature spirits may dwell undisturbed.[19]

He is not alone in leaving a corner of the garden untilled for magical reasons. Mrs M. C. Baker of Weston Turville writes that for many years she has reserved a yard or two of ground round the stump of an old plum tree on which, growing as they please, are stitchwort, bluebells, primroses, windflowers, ferns, periwinkles and a self-sown holly, as 'an atonement for my interference elsewhere in the garden'.

Belief in the efficacy of wild gardens has been given fresh impetus by the growing ecological movement of recent years. Seedsmen have become interested. The Burpee seed company of Warminster, Pa., offer (1976) their 'Woodland Special' mixture to 'transform a shady nook into your own private "Woodland Corner"' with jack-in-the-pulpit, white and purple trillium and roundlobe hepatica! The L. L. Olds Seed Company of Madison, Wisconsin, offer mixed columbines, aspen daisy, wild blue lupins, wild geranium, Indian paintbrush, monkshood and wild forget-me-not. Wintergreen, trailing arbutus, violet, bearberry, wild sweet william and wild bergamot are in the blend sold by Dominion Seed House of Georgetown, Ontario; and in England Nickersons Seed Specialists Ltd of Grimsby, Lincolnshire, put out a 'Nature Conservation Blend' of trefoils and clovers, field lupin, ling heather, broom, ox-eye daisy, foxglove, sleep and white poppies and other wild flowers and grasses, a mixture chosen to improve the condition of the soil and to encourage insects and other wild life.

This growing enthusiasm for wild plants seems to point to a deeper desire than the mere preservation of species, to a more primitive emotion, a desire to draw nearer to nature herself and while, naturally, seedsmen do not suggest that their wild plant mixtures will conciliate the Great Goddess or nature spirits, these plantings would undoubtedly help to create wild gardens favourable for the reception of *devas*. Are not ecologists and those gardeners who favour a little propitiatory magic really talking about precisely the same thing?

6

TRADITIONAL RECEIPTS

This chapter deals with folk-life, less with folklore; with usage, rather than with superstition. Homely fertilizers and receipts for the disposal of pests and diseases, collected by observant gardeners from the Roman period onwards, have never gone out of fashion and interest in them grows year by year. Advice offered in a Canadian publication of 1836 shows the detailed knowledge of such remedies possessed by earlier generations of gardeners:

> Some vegetables are offensive to all insects; such as the elder, especially the dwarf kind, the onion, tansy and tobacco, except to the worm that preys upon that plant. The juice of these may therefore be applied, with effect, in repelling insects; and sometimes the plants themselves, while green, or when reduced to powder, particularly the latter, when made into snuff. Set an onion in the centre of a hill of cucumbers, squashes, melons, etc., and it will effectually keep off the yellow striped bug that preys upon these plants when young.[1]

SOOT AND TEA: BOOTS AND BEER

Soot, central among the gardener's traditional materials, contains nitrogen in the form of ammonium salts. Its application darkens the soil and, useful in cold seasons, allows it to absorb greater heat from the sun. Ted Humphris, head gardener at Aynho, could not overstress the value of soot as a fertilizer for lawns and vegetables: he bought all the soot the local chimney-sweep could provide and often had three one-ton heaps in use. The soot was weathered for a year lest it scorch the plants, then a bucketful was mixed with a barrow-load of leaf soil, the whole passed through a half-inch sieve and applied in early spring as a top dressing.

Mrs Isabelle Wright of East Howle, County Durham, wrote in 1974: 'I take soot from my chimney flues—we still have coal fires—and immerse a bag of it in a large bucket of hot water. This soot water is sprinkled over the onion bed every two weeks. In thirty-six years we have rarely had a bad onion.'[2] William Jones in *The Gardener's Receipt Book* (1858) described soot manure as 'relished' by pineapples, vines, peaches and shrubs and suggested that if lettuce and strawberry beds were bordered by a slate edging (a favourite Victorian decoration) this should be smeared with a paste of 'train oil' (another favourite) and soot, which no snails would cross: 'Sow soot with the peas, and to keep the sparrows from nibbling the young tops as soon as the peas come through the ground, dress the rows with soot when the plants are damp. As soot is one of the richest of manures the crop will be benefitted by its use.' Sprinkling fresh hardwood ashes mixed with fresh soot over gooseberry bushes when the leaves are damp disposes of all caterpillars.

To destroy insect pests of fruit trees a spectacular American receipt of 1805 advised that two shovelsful of soot and one of quicklime be mixed together, laid to windward of the tree and sprinkled with water, when a great cloud of gas would rise into the branches to destroy all insects, without, it was claimed, any damage to the tree itself.[3] The Henry Doubleday Research Association rates soot as a moderately successful slug deterrent which, before the development of derris and DDT, was used also quite effectively against flea-beetle. Its scent checks egg-laying and foliage eating by pests, but as a manure it is inferior to pure sulphate of ammonia.

Thus the enthusiasm of soot's devotees seems rather more marked than that of its evaluators. Is soot's reputation perhaps bolstered by immemorial associations with the family hearth, heart of life and magic: a reputation formed before the onset of chemical gardening? A pocketful of soot was thought protective on an unavoidable night journey: in Europe to this day soot retains a strong reputation in fighting sorcery and in curse-breaking. This could well have been part of its original appeal for gardeners, prudently anxious to save their crops from the evil eye. Soot had highly practical qualities, it is true, which tend to distract the imagination in assessing its value, but no gardener worth his salt turned his back on a bonus of protection from the occult menaces about him. Mrs Stanbury of Holsworthy, Devon, confirms the durability of these emotions: 'My late father, Richard Dockett, always maintained that the common soot *from one's own chimney* was very beneficial in the garden . . .'[4] The special unity between a gardener's hearth and his garden may have meant that soot from such an intimate source had special efficacy.

Every gardener has seen wonderful plants which their owners swear have benefitted from daily applications of tealeaves from the family teapot. In 1974 Mrs Phyllis Mailer of Matfield, Kent, as one of the many, counted over two hundred red blossoms on her twenty-year-old Christmas cactus which she waters every morning with tea. Like leather-dust—in a plastic age far harder to obtain—tealeaves contain tannin, a good organic fertilizer, and, useful as any leaves, add humus to soil. Dried and spread, tealeaves make an excellent mulch, conserving moisture and suppressing weeds. If holes for new trees are dug in advance and the teapot is emptied into them over several months, young trees, especially camellias, benefit. Since the camellia and the tea-plant are both members of the *Theaceae*, there is a clear hint of the old magic tethering a plant and its parts, alive or dead. In the Ozarks, tannin-rich old leather boots are buried near peach trees (the luck-bringing qualities of old shoes probably enhance the charms of this manure). Farmers near Little Rock, Arkansas, have been known to drive miles into town to ransack the garbage dump for discarded boots for their orchards—the older and more decayed the better!

Human urine (rich in nitrogen, phosphoric acid and potash) once held a secure place in the arsenal of home manures. 'I knew a Vine,' wrote Farmer William Ellis of Little Gaddesden, Hertfordshire, in 1772, 'at the Back Door of a Public House, that had a little Bank raised above the Root, in this the Guests frequently piss'd, and it produced more Grapes every year, than any one Vine in these Parts.' Urine was of course more readily available for garden use in the days of the chamber-pot: modern plumbing has changed that. It was certainly a most useful and valued plant stimulant; one informant remembered that when he was 'caught short' in his aunt's garden at Wembley, Middlesex, he was invariably sent over to the runner beans: 'It's good for them!' It was also a way of joining an owner's life-forces to those of his plants: some Illinois gardeners still reckon to urinate every day for a week against the trunk of a newly-planted fruit-tree. In Greece and other Mediterranean countries urine, like all vital secretions, has a high reputation in the treatment of bewitchment. On balance it seems that what would appear today to be a practical use of a handy substance probably once had accepted magical significance.

Gardeners raising prize-winning vegetables sometimes recommend beer as a stimulant, another conviction depending partly upon imitative magic: as people enjoy and grow fat on beer, so will plants. Leslie Leadbetter, a parks department gardener in Shropshire, poured pints of ale from his local pub round a prize cabbage he raised in 1974, which, measuring five feet across at its widest point, was pronounced the world's largest. There is scientific support for the use of beer: brewers' grains may contain 76 per cent water, 1·2 per cent ash, 0·9 per cent nitrogen, 0·5 per cent phosphoric acid and 0·05 per cent potash: the spent wash of distilleries contains notable amounts of nitrogen. Spent hops, wet from the brewery, and malt dust or culms, are also useful.

Another old favourite among manures was made from parings of horses' hooves, to be had from the blacksmith for the asking in the days of the horse. Parings were steeped in a tub of water until they decomposed into a nourishing, if smelly, liquid manure, predecessor of today's hoof and horn meal.

In New England, gypsum or calcium sulphate was a well-known fertilizer of which vast quantities were sowed; it was reputed to be so powerful that, magically, it would draw manure from a neighbour's land, if scattered near his fence. Pennsylvanian Germans favoured gypsum from 1770 when a Pennsylvanian visiting Germany noticed a crop of exceptionally luxuriant clover by a path along which stucco was regularly carried for building, and brought the idea home.[5] Although forgotten today, gypsum's rejection has been fairly recent: Wheeler's *Manures and Fertilizers* (1913), published in New York, contains no fewer than twenty-eight index references to gypsum as a manure.

EGGSHELLS AND ASHES: SOAP AND TOBACCO

'For two years my husband and I grew potatoes and were troubled by the slugs having a feast before we did ... then we were told put crushed eggshells in before we set the potatoes.'[6] In recent years George Modds of Leavesden, Hertfordshire, using applications of mothballs and eggshells, has grown Brussels sprouts nine feet high. For twenty years Mr Modds had tried to grow sprouts without success because of a heavy infection of his soil by clubroot (or 'finger and toe'). He then remembered this traditional remedy mentioned to him as a boy by his Norfolk grandfather, tried it and grew giant, disease-free plants. The success of the remedy is still something of a mystery: Roy Gunton, head of the horticultural department of Oaklands College of Agriculture, St Albans, is reported to have said: 'Something has happened to these giant Brussels which we don't understand.'[7]

In the eighteenth century, wood and coal ashes were applied after lawn mowing to kill slugs and caterpillars, particularly effectively, it was said, if well watered in 'with Piss out of the Chamber Pots'. Pansies rooted well with coal ashes sprinkled about them and a dressing of wood ashes was said to destroy celandines. Seventeenth-century gardeners used potash water and brine on weedy paths. Beatrice Trum Hunter of Hillsborough, New Hampshire, finds that wood ashes spread around cauliflowers, cabbages, peas and onions, control maggots, snails, aphides, clubroot, red spider and bean beetles,[8] and a dusting powder against cabbage worms of one (US) quart of wood ashes, one quart of flour and a cup of table salt is recommended by Tussie M. Jones of West Virginia. The Henry Doubleday Research Association recommends the spreading of wood ashes before sowing broad beans if 'chocolate spot', indicating potash deficiency, is evident.

A border of salty sea sand sprinkled round a garden plot keeps slugs away, and salt sprinkled over heading cabbages displeases caterpillars. Soda scattered about onions reduces the risk of mildew;[9] and powdered alum dusted over fern crowns was a remedy against slugs recommended by J. E. Smith, a noted London fern-grower of the 1920s.[10] In the United States the *Southern Planter* (1842) recommended that a cubic inch of chalk be dissolved in a (US) pint of vinegar, diluted with two pints of water and poured over plants infected with grubs.

Some gardeners believe that shingles soaked in tar hung among branches keep pests from fruit-trees. *The Old Farmer's Almanac* pronounced that no birds would touch seed first dipped in tar and then dusted with lime and plaster before sowing. 'About 1925,' writes a correspondent,

> an old friend of mine, a market gardener who lived at Woodcote Farm, near Fareham, Hampshire, was seen to be drawing a wet sack over a bed of freshly-sown cabbage seed. The sack was soaked in paraffin to drive away cabbage-white butterfly. It did the trick! At the nursery garden where I worked as a boy I saw my boss sow radish seed which he had shaken beforehand in a small bag with some red lead powder. The birds never touched seed so treated.[11]

In the days when the family laundry was done in a kitchen tub with strong yellow soap, washing water was a popular pesticide, particularly used for the white cottage garden lilies and, in America, as a spray against gooseberry mildew. Mrs Stanbury remembers: 'My late grandmother, Mrs Andrews of Lawhitton, near Launceston, always had the most lovely lilies—arum and *regale*—and she always threw her weekly washing water over them—no detergents in those days.'[12] Mrs Wright, a Durham miner's daughter, writes: '. . . at home Dad bathed in the tin bath, oval in shape. The water used was carried over to our allotment each night after back shift and the leeks and everything there watered. When Mam finished washing in the "posstub" that water too was saved for the allotment.'[13]

Today nicotine, a plant alkaloid derived from the tobacco plant, *Nicotiana Tabacum*, is a well-known commercial insecticide, but in earlier days gardeners relied upon their own potions, often using a 'wash' made up by tobacconists from tobacco sweepings and dust. Four ounces of tobacco to one gallon of water was effective against many pests, including mealy cabbage aphis, pea and bean weevils and cabbage-white butterflies. Snuff was also used. Cecil Atkins writes:

> Harry Dormer who lived in Upper Winchendon and died some years ago at the age of 80 spent all his life in the same cottage where he was born, and was a genuine old countryman. In the spring he grew great quantities of Brussels sprouts and cauliflower plants for sale (at 1½d. per score). There were few insecticides then but although many lost their plants through the ravages of fly and flea-beetle this never happened to Harry who had a remedy of his own. He used to mix wood ash and snuff together and put it in a cotton bag. Then, very early in the morning, while the dew was still on the garden, he would walk along his rows of plants and shake the bag just

above them. The fine powder would stick to the little plants which were wet with dew. This was an absolute deterrent, and never failed. I use the same remedy myself now and have always found it to be most successful.

Pennsylvanian gardeners of the eighteenth century believed that water in which potatoes had been boiled would 'completely destroy all insects in every stage of existence, from the egg to the fly',[14] and the truth of this belief may soon be revealed for the HDRA is at present conducting trials with a solution made from potatoes whose skins have turned green through exposure to light. These contain the toxic alkaloid solanine.

THERAPEUTIC PLANTS

Rank-smelling elder draped over fruit trees or cabbage plants keeps insects away, and elder blossoms picked at full moon in June (a touch of the White Goddess's magic) and stuck into fruit drive out weevils. Elder twigs spiked along rows of broad beans will, it is said, hold off the 'black army', 'black dolphin' or 'collier'—aphis or blackfly. Miss P. M. Olver of Cranbrook, Kent, told the writer in 1974: 'I have pushed in a number of elder twigs this year, and have had scarcely any blackfly on the beans, although they have attacked other plants in the garden. The elder does not have to be in flower—I believe that it is the smell of the foliage which counts.'[15] Victorian gardeners recommended elder spray against rose mildew and one modern gardener considers an infusion of elder and yew leaves as effective as—and cheaper than—commercial nicotine against leaf-miner. R. W. Butcher of Billericay, Essex, told the HDRA that his Victoria plum and greengage trees were badly attacked by aphides every year; they looked sick and were covered with a sooty mould. Three pounds of elder leaves were therefore boiled for one hour in a gallon of water, which was strained, mixed with soap flakes and used as a spray at four-week intervals from May onwards, when the year's attack began. 'Within three days the aphis kill was very noticeable . . . the trees had not looked so clean for years.'

Perhaps throwing more light on the 'magical' effects of whipping described earlier was the discovery by a Vermont gardener about 1840 that sweet elder bushes were always free from pests. For many seasons afterwards he 'whipped' the trunks of his choicest Pound Sweet and

Pearmain apples with green elder branches to keep injurious insects away.

Belcher's *Farmers' Almanac for the Province of Nova Scotia* for 1898 recommended that when currant and gooseberry bushes put out their first leaves a sprinkling of white hellebore powder (the powdered rhizome of *Veratrum album*) be applied as soon as the dew was off, against currant worm and gooseberry sawfly. Taking a surprisingly modern stance on the dangers of chemicals, the almanac maintained that the powder was to be strongly preferred to 'Paris green' or 'London purple', two garden poisons then in common use: 'There are homicides as well as insecticides . . .' Hellebore powder (which is still listed among remedies in the *RHS Dictionary*) loses its toxic qualities after exposure to the air for three or four days and may therefore be applied safely to ripening fruit. Another old-fashioned standby against thrips, greenfly and red spider was the burning of laurel leaves in melon pits and greenhouses.

Stinging nettles (*Urtica dioica*), most valuable of weeds, form perfect black humus in growth, which is ideal for seedbeds. Since nettles collect large quantities of nitrogen, silica, iron, chlorophyll, protein, phosphates and other soil salts, liquid feeds including nettles return these valuable substances to treated plants. In 1973 Harold Greenslade of Tunbridge Wells, Kent, was awarded the Lindley Silver Medal of the Royal Horticultural Society and a Certificate of Cultural Commendation for his 'Charm' chrysanthemum, a noble plant sixteen feet six inches in circumference and bearing over 12,000 flowers (Mr Greenslade counted no further). The plant was nurtured on a traditional brew of nettles, soot and sheep manure.

Dr Rudolf Steiner called the nettle the *Allersweltskerl* 'jack of all trades'—because of its versatility in the garden, aiding ailing plants, suppressing pests and, as a 'plant doctor', correcting plant malformations. In one receipt quoted in *Star and Furrow*, nettles cut before flowering are laid in a wooden cask, covered with rain water and left for about a month to ferment before the mixture, diluted 1:10 with rainwater, is sprayed on the soil. Anita Linder reported in *Bio-Dynamics* that in the second half of May 1972 a severe frost scorched her wax beans, which turned black: but after a good dose of nettle manure they quickly recovered and produced an outstanding crop.

Stone fruits or tomatoes packed in nettle leaves are said to keep their bloom for long periods and to travel, ripen and keep better. Maple leaves, too, layered with stored apples, carrots and potatoes have noticeable preservative effects. But in North Carolina, true to plant-affinity magic, they say that fruit should always be packed on its *own* leaves.[16] Plants grown near foxgloves, lilies of the valley and scillas keep more satisfactorily after cutting or harvesting. Rhubarb leaves contain oxalic acid and are therefore poisonous. It is a toxicity put to good use by gardeners. Three pounds of mature leaves boiled in 6 pints of water for 30 minutes, strained, bottled and mixed when used with an ounce of soft soap dissolved in 4 pints of hot water, makes an efficient spray against aphides on roses or apples, or black spot on roses. C. E. Terry writes that his Irish allotment holders drop a handful of rhubarb leaves into a waterbutt and swear by this water as an insecticide.

'When I plant cabbages or Brussels sprouts I put a small piece of rhubarb stem into the hole first. This stops clubroot: and it works. I dressed one row only in this way; only plants with rhubarb stems were unaffected by clubroot,' writes K. R. Cattermole of Watford, whose father was under-gardener to Lady Ela Russell of Chorleywood House, Hertfordshire.[17] The HDRA has concluded that the old remedy does indeed work for many gardeners. In 1973 a report from Liverpool showed that four pieces of rhubarb 1½ inches long, dropped into each hole when seedlings were set out, gave 90 per cent immunity from club root; 5 per cent of the remaining plants showed a trace of the disease; 5 per cent were slightly affected. Untreated control plants were severely diseased. It is hazarded that the oxalic acid in rhubarb leaves (or perhaps another element) halts clubroot zoospores. Many gardeners remember the remedies as being in regular use for over sixty years: they are certainly far older than that.

The onion family is prominent among plant remedies. One long-established receipt requires that chives leaves be infused in boiling water and the liquid, diluted with twice the amount of plain water, be used against gooseberry mildew and apple scab. Water in which a clove of garlic has been steeped for a few hours is strained and sprayed on plants against scale insects. A spray including a 3 per cent extract of garlic powder is said to dispose of mildew and scab in cucumbers, rust in beans and blight in tomatoes. A gardener in Uruguay reports that there, even in 1973—'a lousy year'—plant lice vanished after spraying with a garlic solution. Vines round which seven cloves of garlic were planted did well without the further 'protection' usually thought indispensable. The number seven suggests a touch of the occult.

Major reports on the use of garlic in the garden are those of David Greenstock, *Garlic as a Pesticide* (1970) and, with Querubin Larrea, *Garlic as an Insecticide* (1972). One hundred grams of finely chopped garlic in a litre of water were used as a spray against aphis, cabbage white butterfly, *Hemiptera* on brassicas, *Bruchus pisorum* (a serious menace in Spain, where the experimental work was done) and the Colorado beetle. This solution failed, apparently because of its weakness. But when a 5 per cent emulsion of crude oil of garlic was tried, an 82 per cent field mortality rate among aphides after twenty-four hours and a laboratory mortality of 98 per cent were noted. It was concluded that this emulsion was one of the most powerful plant-extract insecticides so far discovered and that given certain conditions there could be little doubt that essential oil of garlic could be as effective as DDT and similar pesticides—as well as being non-poisonous to men and animals.

These are of course the latest sophisticated scientific opinions but for centuries similar beliefs have permeated country folklore. William Brown writes of his father, the Devon hedger: 'He used to boil wild garlic leaves and put the water over his plants to keep pests away . . .'[18]

MOLES, MICE AND BIRDS

There are a dozen remedies against the tiresomeness of moles. Best known perhaps is the plant *Euphorbia lathyrus*, caper spurge or 'mole plant'. In the *Sunday Telegraph* in 1973 a correspondent commended it warmly: 'This rather dull and self-sowing plant is frowned upon by some professional gardening correspondents but it succeeded where smoke bombs, moth balls and a mole catcher failed.' This testimony is confirmed by Dr W. E. Shewell-Cooper, honorary director of the Good Gardeners' Association, who comments that no mole will go nearer to true caper spurge than 60 feet; but the plant must be two years old and there must be no barrier of any kind, no hedge, path or brick edging, between the plant and the animal. Members of the GGA all over Britain have found that the caper spurge remedy did work perfectly; if it did not, then some barrier, however slight, was to be discovered between plant and mole.[19]

Some recommend that onions, leeks or garlic be laid in moles' runs to drive them away; others rely on slices of burnt red herring, nutmegs, strips of wet newspaper, elder leaves, mothballs or prickly clippings of roses or blackberries. The Elizabethan gardener Thomas Hyll said that if boys were encouraged to play football in the garden the vibrations would frighten the moles, sensitive of hearing. The notion survives and *Mother Earth Catalogue 6*, published in the United States in 1975, offered for sale a small windmill whose clacking vibrations passing into the soil would, it was said, protect a large garden from the depredations of moles or gophers (the North American ground squirrel). Arthur Jarvis of Woodbridge, Suffolk, remembers an East Anglian remedy in use for a century or more and handed down to him by his grandfather: 'Stand pint bottles without corks about 2 or 3 yards apart in the moles' runs. The sound of the wind in the necks of the bottles drives moles away.' *The Old Farmer's Almanac* advocated an empty barrel set upright in the middle of the garden, saying that no groundhog would go near it, although whether because of wind vibrations or appearances was not clear. A single strand of string hung with tarred paper strips is useful against invasive deer, and rabbits will never pass a barricade of onion plants (ornamental alliums do as well) or sticks dipped into brimstone.

In addition to the magic described in chapter two there are more practical remedies against mice and voles. When, in the 1920s, J. S. Gray was working as a private gardener at Alverstoke in Hampshire, his employer told him that her seed peas had all been stolen by fieldmice. Mr Gray spread a bucketful of holly leaves in the seed-drills after sowing the next batch and the trouble ceased forthwith.[20] Many advise soaking peas in paraffin overnight before planting.[21] At Aynho peas were dusted with red lead as a protection before germination; when this took place thorny rose prunings cut into six-inch lengths were laid across the rows. Everlasting pea (*Lathyrus latifolius*) vines laid across plants keeps away field mice and small rodents: so, it is said, does spearmint and dwarf elder. Half a joke, half serious, is the old instruction to 'wash your cat and sprinkle the water over the garden to keep mice away'.[22] Cats are discouraged by thorny blackthorn branches pegged down about invitingly-tilled seedbeds.

As excellent pest destroyers, snakes should by rights be welcome visitors to the garden: still, those who do not care for them might test the Roman belief mentioned by Varro that 'if an oak stake is driven into the middle of a dung hill, no serpent will breed there'.[23] Adders are allegedly deterred by wormwood and southernwood in garden borders, and gardeners of the American South believe that gourds planted round their houses keep snakes away.[24]

Many gardeners hold to the saying, 'No birds, no crops: the labourer is worthy of his hire,' and welcome birds to the garden. But, however valuable they are as controllers of insect pests, fruit-stealing and bud-destruction by certain birds can become a nuisance. Since birds quickly become accustomed to scarers a great many have been devised. Robert Forby in *Vocabulary of East Anglia* (1830) describes the 'feather-pie'—a 'hole in the ground, filled with feathers fixed on strings and kept in motion by the wind. An excellent device to scare birds.' Victorian gardeners relied upon potatoes stuck all over with white feathers and suspended, hawk-like, high above the garden plot by a red thread. This choice of colour was not accidental but magical: red, sacred to Thor, god of lightning, is the prime anti-witch colour and with it Scots farmers tied bunches of protective rowan twigs to their cows' tails, for as everyone knew, 'Rowan tree and red theid, gar the witches tyne their speed.' In the 1920s fruit-growers in New England saved their cherries by hanging jointed toy snakes from the branches of their trees. The writer's Sussex grandmother stood her upended yard broom like a crouching cat among the ripening raspberries. The cherry orchards of the village of Wood Green in the New Forest were notable, and there in season 'cherry bells' hung from every tree to scare birds away. 'As sweet sounding as the cherry bells,' was a local saying.[25] Jacob Verrall, the miller of Rodmell, Sussex, who died in 1918 aged seventy-four, also relied on a bell. He spent the later infirm years of his life in a tiny room overlooking the garden of Monks House. Outside the window was an enormous cherry tree. In the cherry season Verrall lay with one end of a long cord tied to his big toe; the other was attached to a large bell at the top of the tree and, whenever he saw birds approaching, especially in early morning, he jerked his

K

foot and the bell rang out—to an accompaniment of fluttering wings and alarmed cries.[26]

Other gardeners again turn to onions—a favourite bird-scarer of the Chinese garden. K. R. Cattermole writes: 'I have onions on the branches of my peach, apple and pear trees, to stop the birds from pecking the blossoms and eating the fruit.'[27] The monks of Fulda Abbey have found that cloves of garlic suspended in muslin bags from fruit-tree branches send birds shrieking away. This device, of ancient pedigree, is mentioned by Richard Surflet in *La Maison Rustique* (1600), a favourite handbook to French country life of the seventeenth century.

Gardeners continue to catch slugs in half-buried saucers filled with beer, into which the creatures fall: earwigs or church-pigs, sow-bugs in America and zoo-pigs in Devon are trapped in half grapefruit skins or in cucumber rinds laid overnight beneath greenhouse staging. Elizabethan gardeners used hollow canes, even old shoes 'stopt with hay' as traps: one correspondent writes, 'At the last nursery at which I worked they cut a potato in half and scooped out some of the inside as a trap for woodlice in the fernhouse.'[28] In the nineteenth century a favourite remedy was a boiled potato wrapped in dry hay and laid in a flowerpot in the corners where woodlice would congregate. With sticks for handles potatoes buried four inches deep are efficient snares for wireworms: every week potatoes and pests together can be dug up and destroyed.

A strong decoction of elder leaves poured over their nests disposes of ants overnight. The Victorians used wool tied round the trunks of espalier and standard fruit-trees to prevent ants from climbing them and spoiling the fruit. In *Notable Things, Book Four*, Thomas Lupton wrote in the seventeenth century: 'If you stamp Lupins . . . and therewith rub the bottom of any tree, no Ants or Pismires will go up and touch the same tree.' Leonard Mascall recommended: 'Ye shall take of the saw-dust of Oke-wood . . . and strew it about the tree root and the next raine that doth come, all the Pismires or Ants shall die there.' Pepper moves ants on, as it does sparrows. Wasps (eloquently called 'apple-drains' in Devon) are caught in spring in traps baited with the fragrant herb angelica. A saucer of cream laced with toadflax juice is another old-fashioned remedy, said to spell certain death to all kinds of greenhouse flies.

Another plant with which it would be rewarding to experiment in a greenhouse setting is *Nicandra physaloides*, 'the shoo-fly plant', originally from Peru. It has pale lavender-blue flowers with a white centre, and appears in August and September. Dominion Seed House of Canada, who offer its seed, point out that its reputation as a fly-chaser goes back to the early second century AD. It was said that flies would never willingly remain in the same room with the 'shoo-fly', although some modern experimenters have expressed doubts. The characteristic causing the deterrent effect is not obvious: neither leaves nor flowers have detectable odour.

PLANTS FOR BEES AND BUTTERFLIES

In earlier years beekeeping and gardening marched more closely together than they do today, and a body of folklore concerns garden plants especially pleasing to bees, whose contented presence was an asset to both house and garden. Bees are still of course most valuable pollinators, and today an increasing number of gardeners are coming to enjoy beekeeping again.

'Hyssop planted near to bee hives is said to give a good flavour to honey,' writes F. W. Baty. Bees have a great fondness for thyme also, and the thyme slopes of Mount Hymettus near Athens give a world-famous fragrance to its honey. Catnip or nepeta, salvia, marjoram, basil, coriander, dill, savory, mint and blue-flowered borage or 'bee-bread', in flower, are other bee favourites and 'Mignonette is a plant of which you cannot sow too much,' wrote a nineteenth-century bee-keeper: 'No one who has tasted mignonette honey would wish to have better.'[29]

Best known of all bee plants is balm, which Varro called melli-fluously 'honey-leaf', 'bee-leaf' or 'bee-herb'. John Parkinson, the Elizabethan gardener, wrote: 'It is also a herbe wherein Bees doe much delight, as hath beene found by experience of those that have kept great store; if the Hives be rubbed on the inside with some thereof, ... it draweth by the smell thereof to resort thither ...'

There are as many 'butterfly plants' as 'bee plants'. The seedsmen Thompson and Morgan of Ipswich offer a special 'English country flowers' seed mixture to attract butterflies, which particularly like kentranthus, or 'Pretty Betsy', sedum, Michaelmas daisy, scabious, lilac, honesty, cornflower, clover, hyssop, forget-me-not, thyme, lavender and muscari bluebell. Best known of all is the mauve-tasselled buddleia, called the 'butterfly bush' in America. And Mrs N. C. Frampton writes of a lesser-known yet equally magnetic plant: 'I come from Dorset . . . my mother used to "call the butterflies": this she did by waving a sprig of lobelia in the air. I have seen her with a cloud of tortoiseshell butterflies about her.'[30]

7

COMPANION PLANTING

Valuable indeed are 'companion plants' which encourage or inhibit their neighbours' health and productivity. Plants may provide shelter, enrich the soil or control weeds: perhaps most important of all are plants whose root and leaf excretions and scents seem to repel harmful insects. Since the earliest days of gardening the mysterious affinities and antipathies of the plant world have commanded the gardener's attention: 'For instance,' wrote Varro, the Roman agriculturalist,' . . . large numbers of large walnut trees close by render the border of the farm sterile'; an observation echoed by Mrs H. Lamoureux of Kelowna, British Columbia, who writes that when her family farmed in south-western Ontario, near Kitchener, about 1950, the belief was widespread that no plants would grow in the shade of the fabled North American 'black walnut'. Horticulturalists have found that the roots of the black walnut do indeed secrete a substance harmful to other plants. In companion planting, personal experiment is an essential, for soil and season, climate and country, the strain and vitality of pests and predators, all vary greatly: companionages that succeed brilliantly in one season may fail dismally in another. The old-fashioned cottage garden, remembered with such nostalgia today, probably owed its exuberant undisciplined beauty to a rich and random tapestry of flowers, fruits and vegetables— to unconscious 'companion planting' because, left to her own devices, nature seldom if ever contrives neat areas of one species alone. Future gardeners seem certain to regard as sadly mistaken today's trend towards monoculture on farm and in garden.

HERBS

Soft in colours and spicy in scents, herbs have always provided the traditional border for the vegetable garden, where their pungency is widely held to deter pests and to stimulate vegetable neighbours to better performance. Borage, lavender, hyssop, sage, parsley, rosemary, chervil, tarragon, chives, thyme, marjoram, dill, basil, chamomile and lovage are all good neighbours. Exceptions to this general beneficence are wormwood and fennel of the green and bronze feathery leaves:

> *Sow Fennel*
> *Sow trouble*

is the cautious little rhyme, for fennel appears to seriously retard the growth of many plants, with the curious exception, it is said, of *Eremurus*, the foxtail lily.

There are many testimonies as to the amiability of herbs. 'My father used to grow fine roses in Cornwall many years ago,' writes Mrs Margaret Knight. 'He always insisted on their being grown near "boy's love" or southernwood. "They'll not do well anywhere else," he said. They did not!'[1] The therapeutic chamomile, 'the doctor', cures the ailing. Yarrow enhances the essential oils of herbs near it and marjoram the flavour of neighbouring vegetables. Parsley is an obliging friend to roses, tomatoes and asparagus. William Coles in *The Art of Simpling* (1656) wrote of an ancient companionage: 'Among strawberries sow here and there some Borage seed and you shall find the strawberries under those leaves farre more larger than their fellowes.' Tusser had noticed another:

> *The Gooseberry, Respis* [raspberry] *and Roses all three,*
> *With Strawberries under them trimly agree.*

THE ALLIUM FAMILY

The allium family enlarges its remedial reputation: 'My late good Father always set a row of onions between every row of carrots,' writes Mrs O'Regan from County Cork. 'This he claimed—quite rightly—would mean that he was never troubled with carrot pests.'[2] Interplanted garlic (itself significantly free from pests) repels onion fly and leek moth. In September 1975 W. Clayworth of Rotorva, New Zealand, told *Garden News* that he had planted garlic round four rose bushes heavily infected with black spot: as the garlic grew the black spot vanished, only to reappear as the garlic died away towards the season's end. Scientists concur: the University of California Entomological Research Station at Riverside confirms the effectiveness of garlic against insect pests, especially the pests of raspberries and grapes.

Bulgarian farmers growing roses for the production of attar of roses have long been aware that neighbouring alliums increase the potency of this essential oil. Confidence in the effect is widespread, and Thomas Hardy recorded the Dorset custom of planting an onion beside a rose bush to 'make the roses smell sweeter'. Chives growing beneath apple trees are widely believed to reduce scab, and Mrs M. C. Baker writes of her wall-trained peach-tree, Amsden June, in Buckinghamshire: 'The year after I planted the chives round the tree there was a little "leaf fire" but as that year (1971) wore on the tree looked healthier and healthier and this year (1973) I picked off three or four diseased leaves only and the tree seems to be in excellent shape.'[3]

During the experiments reported in *Garlic as a Pesticide* David Greenstock sowed alternate rows of garlic and onions and over a three-year period 98 per cent of the onions came up without blemish. It was clearly shown that garlic set between onion rows practically eliminated the ravages of onion fly. The rank odour of garlic might seem to be the obvious protective element but Mgr Greenstock concluded that the repellent effect actually lies in a root secretion.

<h2 style="text-align:center">COMPANION FLOWERS</h2>

For centuries gardeners have regarded the cheerful marigold, *Calendula officinalis*, as a good companion. A correspondent in *Garden News*, September 1975, wrote that he had had self-sown marigolds growing everywhere on his allotment—and no fly pests at all. Marigolds of all kinds are thought valuable, but for the past twenty years attention has focussed specifically on *Tagetes*, a genus of some thirty species: *T. erecta*, the African marigold; *T. lucida*, the Mexican marigold; *T. patula*, the French marigold; and *T. minuta*, an annual from South America with clusters of small pale yellow flowers. *Tagetes* was sacred to the agricultural gods of Equador and pre-Inca Peru, and with its aid potatoes, runner beans, sweet potatoes, sweet corn, French beans and tomatoes were grown on the same irrigated terraces for hundreds of years. Without its use there seems little doubt that eelworms, attracted by such intensive and persistent cultivation, would have quickly destroyed the crops. The 'discovery' in the 1960s of the virtues of *Tagetes* was accidental and occurred when a Dutch nurseryman named Berg-Smit grew *T. erecta* as a cut flower crop following daffodils and found that eelworm damage was greatly reduced. Root secretions of *Tagetes* are said to kill eelworm (or nematodes) at a distance of three feet. When *Tagetes* was planted as a cover crop in Alabama and Georgia a dramatic fall in the nematode population was noted.

The Henry Doubleday Research Association favours *T. minuta* for deterrent use since its secretions are far stronger than those of garden varieties. In trials *Tagetes* has proved its worth against potato eelworm and, in the Cheddar Valley of Somerset, against strawberry eelworm. *The 1961 Tagetes Experiment* (1962) recorded HDRA findings to that date, and research has continued. As a bonus *Tagetes* is said to suppress the growth of such nuisances as couch grass, ground elder, bindweed ('by Gardeners in wrath called the Devil's Guts') and thistles, as well as wireworms, keeled slugs, millepedes and the fungus diseases of potatoes and tomatoes. Lady Eleanor Sinclair of Windsor Park, Belfast, wrote in 1974: 'If you grow pots of French marigolds among your greenhouse plants there will be no greenfly. My head gardener did this and it always worked.'[4]

Thousands of gardeners believe that nasturtiums trained up, or growing under, apple trees will save the trees from woolly aphis or American blight. In his *Agricultural Course* Dr Steiner recommended nasturtiums against whitefly. Mrs Stanbury writes of a less familiar companionage: 'An old uncle of mine told me that should you be inundated with docks, plant phlox and the docks will soon disappear "as they do not bed down together".'[5] Florists are also aware of companionages and use them in their work: Bill Emerson, gardener at Government House, Winnipeg, reports that tulips suffer from being near daffodils and takes care to keep the plants well apart in his greenhouses and displays.

Narcissi and lilies of the valley put together in a bouquet soon wither; and mignonette in a vase causes other flowers to wilt.

The many companionages of the vegetable garden are well established; and new ones constantly come to light. Peas and beans are inimical to the onion family and grow wretchedly in company with its members but flourish by carrots, beetroot and cauliflower. Gladioli are said to have a strongly adverse effect on the growth of peas and beans, even at a distance of fifty feet. Gooseberry bushes with broad beans nearby are likely to be free from caterpillars. In September 1975 another *Garden News* reader, R. Harvey of Norwich, suggested that a dozen sweetpea plants be planted among runner beans in the second week in June: the fragrance of sweetpea flowers attracts bees to the beans and improves pollination, thus reducing bud drop and improving the crop yield.

Amateur Gardening was told in November 1975 by P. J. Long that an acquaintance of his who grew pumpkins for harvest festival decorations had inadvertently planted a pumpkin among his vegetable marrows, with striking results. Ten fruits from one plant weighed an average of 45 pounds each, although the usual weight from the garden was only about 15 pounds. Mr Long added that when he was growing calabash gourds experimentally he recalled the advice of an old West Indian gardener who said that they should be planted alongside marrows, a companionage which was to turn out as effective in Cambridge as it had been in the West Indies. Gourds appear to like to grow with certain other members of the *Cucurbitaceae*, although one Georgia gardener who grew cucumbers next to his calabashes found the cucumbers (although beautifully shaped) so bitter as to be inedible. He blamed cross-pollination.

Cabbages companioned by dill enjoy improved health. Chamomile, southernwood, mint, peppermint, thyme, sage, hyssop, and rosemary repel the cabbage-white butterfly. Lupton in *Notable Things: Book Six* wrote of an antipathy which is still remembered: 'Coleworts [brassicas] are so contrary in nature the one to the other, that they ought not be sown nigh together.' Tomatoes on the other hand are sympathetic to all the cabbage family and repel the cabbage-white butterfly. But again cabbages and strawberries are antipathetic and should be kept far apart.

Mrs Hart of Dinas Powis, Glamorgan, told the HDRA that she had sowed coriander, caraway and aniseed round her carrots and, although the preceding fine summer should by rights have favoured the carrot fly, she had enjoyed her best carrot crop for thirteen years. An exudation of the carrot's roots has been found to assist peas. Dill permitted to bloom nearby greatly reduces a carrot crop: chives, onions and leeks companion carrots well, promoting growth and flavour and suppressing the carrot fly, which also dislikes rosemary, salsify, wormwood, sage and other aromatic herbs.

Gardeners should take particular care to place potatoes and onions, noted enemies, at opposite ends of the garden. Old gardeners in the Ozarks say that onions 'make the 'tater cry its eyes out!'. Horseradish, notably symbiotic with potatoes, is an excellent corner planting for the potato patch. Sweetcorn and potatoes or broad beans and potatoes are reliably said to do well together. American gardeners have heeded this arrangement from the early days of the biodynamic movement and find that it frees the potato from the Colorado beetle and the beans from the bean beetle. George Corrin, consultant to the Bio-Dynamic Agricultural Association has remarked that gardeners have had long years in which to test the veracity of this symbiosis: the first literary reference to it, made by William Speechly in 1779, recommended planting potatoes eighteen inches apart in rows three feet apart, with broad beans between the rows. Potatoes grown near sunflowers, tomatoes, cherries, raspberries, pumpkins or cucumbers are said to be less resistant to late blight. A notable antipathy exists between potatoes and apples: it is a New England tradition that potatoes and apples must never be stored together in the same root cellar or the apples will lose their flavour while the potatoes develop an 'off' quality and rot easily.[6]

Tomatoes, today perhaps the most popular of all garden crops, appreciate the near presence of borage, basil and balm, and like many other crops will keep better if grown near the stinging nettle. Friendship exists between tomatoes and asparagus: outdoor tomatoes should be set by the perennial asparagus. In perhaps the first recorded example of companion planting, early settlers in America found that the Indians grew sweetcorn and pumpkins in alternating rows, the tall corn giving welcome shelter to the recumbent gourd. This combination continues to be just as popular today.

APPENDIX:
THE CALENDAR CHANGE OF 1752

In 1752 the Gregorian calendar replaced the Julian calendar in England and North America. The 'New Style' was adopted under 24 Geo II and in September 1752 eleven days were dropped; 2 September was followed immediately by 14 September. There was resentment: people felt, quite falsely, that they had been deprived of rightful life and those responsible for the change were for years greeted in the streets with cries of 'Give us back our eleven days!' Not all became reconciled. An old Warwickshire labourer who remembered the change of style told his vicar: '. . . depend on it, sir, the nation has never prospered since the style was changed . . . the cuckoo and the swallow and everything else, they don't care for the change. They all come and go by the *old time* and not by the new.' Even late in the nineteenth century people remembered the rhyme:

> *Barnaby Bright, Barnaby Bright,*
> *Longest day and shortest night,*

for St Barnabas' Day, 11 June Old Style, answered to 22 June, about the time of the solstice. It is necessary to bear the two styles in mind when considering the traditional calendar beliefs of the garden.

REFERENCES

1: MOON, SUN AND STARS

(L = *Personal letter 1973–76*)

1 Arthur S. Webster, Norwich, Norfolk (L)
2 Arthur S. Webster, Norwich, Norfolk (L)
3 C. L. Anstine, Marietta, Georgia (L)
4 R. Winder, Caister St Edmund, Norfolk (L)
5 Mrs K. A. Gosling, Hawkchurch, Devon (L)
6 Mrs Evelyne E. Bowes, Burton Lazars, Leicestershire (L)
7 E. Kidd, Guisborough, Yorkshire (L)
8 H. J. Baker, Weston-super-Mare, Avon (L)
9 G. B. Millington, Warley, Worcestershire (L)
10 Azzi, G., *Agricultural Ecology*, 1956, 123
11 Creighton, Helen, *Bluenose Magic: Popular Beliefs and Superstitions in Nova Scotia*, Toronto, 1968, 271
12 Mrs A. Elliott, Norwich, Norfolk (L)
13 Mrs D. Keel, Chew Stoke, Somerset (L)
14 Mrs M. Jones, Broomfield, Essex (L)
15 Arthur S. Webster, Norwich, Norfolk (L)
16 Katie Huss, Annapolis, Maryland (L)
17 Mrs M. Stanbury, Holsworthy, Devon (L)
18 Hoffman, W. J., 'Folklore of the Pennsylvanian Germans', *Journal o American Folklore*, 1888, v 1, 125–35
19 John Temple, Vancouver, British Columbia (L)
20 Mrs P. Gasquet, Boston, Massachusetts (L)
21 Viscount Scarsdale, Kedleston, Derbyshire (L)
22 Cooke, Doris C. ed., 'An Elizabethan Guernseyman's Manuscript Book of Gardening and Medical Secrets', in *The Channel Islands Annual Anthology 1972–1973*, Guernsey, 1972, 27
23 Crouch, W. T. ed., *Culture in the South*, Chapel Hill, NC, 1934, 383
24 Henry X. Banks, St Paul, Minnesota (L)

25 Courtney, M. A., *Cornish Feasts and Folk-Lore*, Penzance, 1890, 169

26 Christopher Sansom, Godalming, Surrey (L)

27 Ed Zeller, Des Moines, Iowa (L)

28 Mrs M. Kruger, Oak Park, Illinois (L)

29 Kopal, Z., *The Moon*, NY, 1960, 60

30 Jefferies, Richard, *An English Village*, Boston, 1904, 340

31 Parker, Derek, *The Question of Astrology*, 1970, 143–55

32 Thun, Maria, 'Use of the Silica Preparation, Thoughts and Lessons', trans by Nancy Hummel from *Lebendige Erde*, *Star and Furrow*, Autumn 1973, 12

33 R. W. Smith, Maghull, Lancashire (L)

34 Hugh W. K. Wilson, Poulton-Le-Fylde, Lancashire (L)

35 Mrs Evelyne E. Bowes, Burton Lazars, Leicestershire (L)

36 Mrs A. F. Smith, Patchway, Bristol (L)

37 Mrs M. Coburn, Harpenden, Hertfordshire (L)

38 *Globe and Mail* (Toronto), 6 March 1975, W4

39 Kenneth R. Cattermole, Watford, Hertfordshire (L)

40 St Clair, Sheila, *Folklore of the Ulster People*, Cork, 1971, 89

41 Wigginton, Eliot ed., *The Foxfire Book*, NY, 1972, 212–27

42 Thun, Maria, 'Nine Years Observations of Cosmic Influences on Annual Plants', trans by Otto Pullich from *Lebendige Erde*, *Star and Furrow*, Spring 1964, 1–7

43 *God's Way*, published by T. E. Black, PO Box 785, Andalusia, Alabama, 36420, USA: Price (1975) $2.00 plus postage. 22 pages. Ready by 15 November each year for following year

2: GROWING MAGIC

1 D. Trebilcock, Greensboro, North Carolina (L)

2 F. A. Welti, Blechingley, Surrey (L)

3 Mrs E. C. Longman, Ferndown, Dorset (L)

4 Nicolson, Harold, *Diaries and Letters 1939–45*, 1968, 450

5 Ed Rogers, Ann Arbor, Michigan (L)

6 Frank J. Taylor, Birmingham, Warwickshire(L)

7 Mrs R. St Leger-Gordon, Sticklepath, Devon (L); Mrs R. Croysdale, Cadeleigh, Devon (L)

8 Ms Esther Schwarz, Wilmington, Delaware (L)

9 W. Walton, Garton-on-the-Wolds, Yorkshire (L)

10 F. W. Baty, Longhope, Gloucestershire (L)

11 'Some Curiosities of Tree-Planting', *Chambers Journal*, 6 September 1873, 575–6

12 Newell, William Wells, 'Conjuring Rats', *Journal of American Folklore*, 1893, 4, xvi, Jan–Mar, 23–32

13 Lyons, Delphine C., *Everyday Witchcraft*, NY 1972, 54

14 Jean C. Thompson, Jacksonville, Florida (L)

15 Wallace Harrison, Lexington, Kentucky (L)

16 Hadfield, Miles, *One Man's Garden*, 1966, 24

17 Randolph, Vance, *Ozark Magic and Folklore*, NY, 1964, 39

18 Charlie Ross, Barmby Moor, Yorkshire (L)

19 Bush, Raymond, *Tree Fruit Growing: Vol 1: Apples*, 1943, 30

20 Randolph, Vance, 'Nudity and Planting Customs', *Journal of American Folklore*, 1953, 333–4

21 Coffin, Tristram P. and Cohen, Hennig, *Folklore in America*, NY, 1966, 139, 239

22 Bancroft, H. H., *Native Races of the Pacific States*, 1856–76, ii, 719; iii, 507

23 Mrs P Gosselin, Chicago, Illinois (L)

24 O'Sullivan, S., *Irish Folk Custom and Belief*, Dublin, n.d., 20

25 F. A. Welti, Blechingley, Surrey (L); Blum, R. and E., *The Dangerous Hour*, 1970, 304

26 Hone, William, *The Every-Day Book*, 1826, 1, 619

27 E. J. Pollet, Baton Rouge, Louisiana (L); Mrs M. Myers, Chalfont St Peter, Buckinghamshire (L)

28 Mrs M. Stanbury, Holsworthy, Devon (L)

29 Miss Marjorie Boulton, Oxford, Oxfordshire (L)

30 Fallow, T. M., *Memorials of Old Yorkshire*, 1909, 302

3: SEASONS AND SAINTS' DAYS

1   Mrs R. Darlington, Poynton, Cheshire (L)

2   Mrs F. S. Edwards, Walsgrave, Coventry (L)

3   *Whitaker's Almanac*, 1973, 1038

4   Mrs Pat Hinnegan, Limerick, Munster (L)

5   H. H. Fletcher, Ely, Cambridgeshire (L)

6   Randell, Arthur, *Sixty Years a Fenman*, 1966, 95

7   Mrs N. O'Regan, Skibbereen, Co Cork, Eire (L)

8   Jane Hetty Duff, Norfolk, Virginia (L)

9   William Hamilton, Richmond, Virginia (L)

10 K. H. Walpole, Heacham, Norfolk (L)

11 R. M. Long, Newport, Monmouthshire (L)

12 Mrs E. Spink, Ruislip, Middlesex (L)

13 E. O. Moss, Launceston, Cornwall (L)

14 Thomas Porlier, New Orleans, Louisiana (L)

15 Mrs R. St Leger-Gordon, Sticklepath, Devon (L); Mrs Cecil Hardwicke, Uploders, Dorset (L)

16 Miss A. M. Trump, Broadclyst, Devon (L)

17 L. Studley, Beaminster, Dorset (L)

18 S. S. Goldschmidt, Cincinnati, Ohio (L)

19   Miss P. J. Rimmer, Oxton, Cheshire (L); John Brake, Liverpool, Lancashire (L)
20   W. Walton, Garton-on-the-Wolds, Yorkshire (L)
21   Christopher Sansom, Godalming, Surrey (L)
22   Mrs B. Miller, Wolverhampton, Staffordshire (L)
23   Miss J. M. Midworth, Lincoln, Lincolnshire (L); N. J. Hinton, Cowley, Oxfordshire (L)
24   Mrs I. Rowland, Wells, Somerset (L); Kenneth W. Samuels, Kenilworth, Warwickshire (L)
25   Mrs Ivy Hysted, Maidstone, Kent (L)
26   Miss E. Reynolds, Upton Snodsbury, Worcestershire (L)
27   Mrs M. Myers, Chalfont St Peter, Bucks (L)
28   Miss P. M. Olver, Cranbrook, Kent (L)
29   Charles Pilley, San Francisco, California (L)
30   Miss W. R. Bush, Câtel, Guernsey (L)
31   Blythe, Ronald, *Akenfield*, 1972, 77–9
32   Mrs E. Gallie, Penmaenmawr, Carnarvonshire (L)
33   Mrs M. Beardshaw, Treswell, Nottinghamshire (L)
34   Robert Parfitt, Beccles, Suffolk (L)
35   K. H. Walpole, Heacham, Norfolk (L); Mrs E. Gallie, Penmaenmawr, Carnarvonshire (L)
36   Mrs I. Wright, East Howle, County Durham (L)
37   Peter Venegas, Baltimore, Maryland (L)
38   O. S. Lines, Oxford, Oxfordshire (L)
39   Mrs M. H. Clark, Throwleigh, Devon (L); Miss P. M. Olver, Cranbrook, Kent (L)
40   J. Foster, Crowland, Peterborough (L)
41   Christopher Sansom, Godalming, Surrey (L)
42   F. T. C. White, Toronto, Ontario (L)
43   Roy Bruce, Oxford, Oxfordshire (L); O. S. Lines, Oxford, Oxfordshire (L)
44   Mrs Janet S. Cox, Wendover, Bucks (L)
45   'Gooseberry Shows', *Chambers Journal*, 15 July 1837, 200; Mead, Harry, 'The Great Gooseberry Contest', *In Britain*, August 1972, 26–7
46   Dr Ruth C. Freeman, Alresford, Hants (L)
47   Ms Bernice Fuller, Traverse City Chamber of Trade, Michigan (L)
48   Peter Sutcliffe, Valley Cottage, New York (L)

4: WITCHCRAFT AND THE SUPERNATURAL

1   Harland, John and Wilkinson, T. T., *Lancashire Folk-Lore*, 1867, 69; Letter from Thomas Hardy to Edward Clodd, read at meeting of The Folk-Lore Society, November, 1896

2 J. Higgins, Boston, Massachusetts (L)
3 Fred Carter, Mullingar, County Westmeath, Eire (L); *Daily Telegraph*, 27 July 1974, 9
4 Zincke, F. B., *Some Materials for the History of Wherstead*, Ipswich, 1887, 178
5 *Notes and Queries*, 30 November 1895, ser 8, v 8, 431–2
6 Dorson, Richard, *America in Legend*, New York, 1973, 22; Burne, C. S., *Shropshire Folk-Lore*, 2v 1883, reprinted Wakefield, 1973, 114,
7 Green, Andrew, *Our Haunted Kingdom*, 1973, 253
8 Courtney, M. A., *Cornish Feasts and Folk-Lore*, Penzance, 1890, 79–80
9 MacManus, D., *Irish Earth-Folk*, NY, 1959, 162–4
10 Christopher Sansom, Godalming, Surrey (L)
11 Mrs M. Stanbury, Holsworthy, Devon (L)
12 Mrs D. P. Read, Powerstock, Dorset (L)
13 Burne, C. S., *Shropshire Folk-Lore*, 2v 1883, 1, 253
14 Mrs Winifred D. Alderton, Lowestoft, Suffolk (L)
15 Mrs M. Stanbury, Holsworthy, Devon (L)
16 Henderson, William, *Notes on the Folk-Lore of the Northern Counties of England and the Borders*, 1866, 189
17 Peter Deegan, San Francisco, California (L)
18 Coats, Alice M., *Garden Shrubs and Their Histories*, 1963, 127; Rasey, Ruth M., *Out of the Saltbox*, NY, 1962, 18
19 William Brown, Stockleigh Pomeroy, Devon (L)
20 Mrs Elsie V. Longman, Ferndown, Dorset (L)
21 Drake, Samuel Adams, *A Book of New England Legends and Folklore*, Boston, 1902, 303–4, quoting Hannah F. Gould's 'The Old Elm of Newbury'
22 Eland, G., *The Chilterns and the Vale*, 1911, 55; Jekyll, Gertrude, *Old West Surrey*, 1904, 39; White, Gilbert, *The Natural History of Selborne*, 1875 ed, 10
23 C. E. Terry, Osmaston Park Allotments Association Ltd, Derby (L)
24 Mrs R. Darlington, Poynton, Cheshire (L)
25 Baïracli-Levy, Juliette de, *Wanderers in the New Forest*, 1958, 125–6
26 Viscount Scarsdale, Kedleston, Derbyshire (L); Michael Trinick, National Trust, Saltram, Devon (L)
27 Mrs M. Hayes, Blackrock, County Dublin, Eire (L)
28 Evans, E. Estyn, *Irish Folkways*, 1957, 101
29 Mrs A. F. Smith, Patchway, Bristol (L); Friend, Hilderic, *Flowers and Flower Lore*, 1886, 10–11
30 Leland, Charles Godfrey, *Gypsy Sorcery and Fortune Telling*, 1891, 153

5: PLANTS, PERSONALITIES AND PREDICTIONS

1 Mrs S. Vinner, Syracuse, New York (L)

2 Joseph Rose, Fredericksburg, Virginia (L)
3 Nichols, Beverley, *Garden Open Today*, 1963, 79–83
4 Kraft, Ken and Pat, *Luther Burbank; the Wizard and the Man*, NY, 1967, 127–31
5 Mrs M. C. Baker, Weston Turville, Buckinghamshire (L); Mrs M. Myers, Chalfont St Peter, Buckinghamshire (L)
6 Mrs Elsie V. Longman, Ferndown, Dorset (L)
7 *Globe and Mail* (Toronto), 24 January 1974, W10
8 T. Schneider, Zurich, Switzerland (L)
9 Moore, Thomas, *Life of Lord Byron*, 1, 1830, 101, quoted by Frazer, J. G., *The Golden Bough*, 12v 1913–15, 166
10 Mrs E. Voll, Bonn, Germany (L)
11 Marcus P. Duff, Yonkers, New York (L)
12 Farrer, J. A., 'Comparative Folklore', *Cornhill Magazine*, January–June, 1876, 44
13 *Notes and Queries*, ser 1, 10, 1854, 461
14 Plimmer, Charlotte and Denis, 'Capability Fred', *In Britain*, November 1974, 11–13
15 Mrs L. Goudman, Cardiff, Glamorgan (L); C. E. Terry, Osmaston Park Allotments Association Ltd, Derby (L); G. B. Millington, Warley, Worcestershire (L); Mrs M. Hayes, Blackrock, County Dublin, Eire (L)
16 Mrs E. Cheshire, Littlehampton, Sussex (L)
17 *Montreal Gazette*, 17 March 1975, 10
18 Mrs M. Knight, Weston-super-Mare, Avon (L)
19 Cowley, Mike, 'There are Fairies at the Bottom of Your Garden', *Canadian Weekend Magazine*, 9 June 1973, 2–4

6: TRADITIONAL RECEIPTS

1 *Cook Not Mad, or Rational Cookery & Sundry Information of Importance to Housekeepers in General*, Kingston, Ontario, 1836, unpaginated
2 Mrs I. Wright, East Howle, County Durham (L)
3 Sloane, Eric, *Diary of an Early American Boy: Noah Black 1805*, NY, 1962, 55
4 Mrs M. Stanbury, Holsworthy, Devon (L)
5 Reaman, G. E., *The Trail of the Black Walnut*, Toronto, 1957, 135–6; Johnson, Clifton, *What They Say in New England*, NY, 1963, 55
6 Mrs C. Cook, Bolton, Lancashire (L)
7 C. E. Terry, Osmaston Park Allotments Association Ltd, Derby (L)
8 *Organic Gardening*, August 1972, 102, Beatrice Trum Hunter, Hillsborough, New Hampshire
9 E. Rose, Amesbury, Wiltshire (L)
10 Smith, J. E., *Ferns! Ferns!*, c 1923, 53

11 J. S. Gray, Fareham, Hampshire (L)
12 Mrs M. Stanbury, Holsworthy, Devon (L)
13 Mrs I. Wright, East Howle, County Durham (L)
14 *The Parlour Portfolio; or, Post-Chaise Companion*, v ii, 1820, 313
15 Miss P. M. Olver, Cranbrook, Kent (L)
16 G. Badoni, Worcester, New Hampshire (L)
17 K. R. Cattermole, Watford, Hertfordshire (L)
18 William Brown, Stockleigh Pomeroy, Devon (L)
19 *Sunday Telegraph*, 25 February 1973, Vivian Ellis, Holnicote, Somerset;
    Daily Telegraph, 31 May 1973, Dr W. E. Shewell-Cooper, Good Garden-
    ers' Association, Arkley, Hertfordshire
20 J. S. Gray, Fareham, Hampshire (L)
21 Mrs A. E. Pepper, Derby (L)
22 N. A. Bennett, Waltham Cross, Hertfordshire (L)
23 Cato, Marcus Porcius and Varro, Marcus Terentius, *De Re Rustica: On
    Agriculture*, 1934, 265
24 P. Woodward, Hot Springs, Arkansas (L)
25 Baïracli-Levy, Juliette de, *Wanderers in the New Forest*, 1958, 109
26 Woolf, Leonard, *Beginning Again: an Autobiography of the Years 1911–1918*,
    1972, 64
27 K. R. Cattermole, Watford, Hertfordshire (L)
28 J. S. Gray, Fareham, Hampshire (L)
29 Cotton, William Charles, *My Bee Book*, 1842, 103
30 Mrs N. C. Frampton, Stevenage, Hertfordshire (L)

7: COMPANION PLANTING

1 Mrs M. Knight, Weston-super-Mare, Avon (L)
2 Mrs N. O'Regan, Skibbereen, County Cork (L)
3 Mrs M. C. Baker, Weston Turville, Buckinghamshire (L)
4 Lady Eleanor L. Sinclair, Windsor Park, Belfast, Ulster (L)
5 Mrs M. Stanbury, Holsworthy, Devon (L)
6 Patrick Byron, Manchester, New Hampshire (L)

BIBLIOGRAPHY

Baker, Margaret, *Discovering the Folklore of Plants*, Tring, 1969

Baker, Margaret, *The Folklore and Customs of Rural England*, Newton Abbot, 1974

Bergen, Fanny D. ed, *Current Superstitions Collected from the Oral Tradition of English Speaking Folk*, Boston, 1896

The Frank C. Brown Collection of North Carolina Folklore, ed N. I. White, 7v, Durham, NC, 1952

Burpee's Farm Annual: 1888, Garden, Farm and Flower Seed, Philadelphia, 1888

Cato, Marcus Porcius and Varro, Marcus Terentius: *De Re Rustica: On Agriculture*, Cambridge, Mass, 1934

Choice Notes from 'Notes and Queries'—Folklore, 1859

Frazer, J. G., *The Golden Bough: A Study in Magic and Religion*, 1911–15, 12v

Graves, Robert, *The White Goddess*, 1961

Hills, Lawrence D., *Pest Control Without Poisons*, Braintree, 1964

Hills, Lawrence D., *Fertility Without Fertilizers*, Braintree (undated)

Hyatt, Henry Middleton, *Folk-Lore from Adams County, Illinois*, New York, 1935

Inwards, R., *Weather Lore*, 4th ed, 1950

Jones, William, *The Gardener's Receipt Book and Treasury of Interesting Facts and Practical Information Useful in Horticulture*, 4th ed, 1858

Kolisko, L., *The Moon and the Growth of Plants*, 1938

Legey, Françoise, *The Folklore of Morocco*, trans Lucy Hotz, 1935

Northall, G. F., *English Folk-Rhymes*, 1892

Parkinson, John, *Paradisi in Sole Paradisus Terrestris*, 1629

Philbrick, Helen and Gregg, Richard B., *Companion Plants and How to Use Them*, 1967

Randolph, Vance, *Ozark Magic and Folklore*, 1947, reprinted New York, 1964

The Royal Horticultural Society Dictionary of Gardening, 3rd ed, Oxford 1965, 4 v

Stout, Earl J. ed, *Folklore from Iowa*, New York, 1936

Sullivan, S., *Irish Folk Custom and Belief*, Dublin (undated)

Thomas, Daniel Lindsey and Lucy Blayney, *Kentucky Superstitions*, Princeton, NJ, 1920

Tompkins, Peter and Bird, Christopher, *The Secret Life of Plants*, New York, 1972

Tusser, Thomas: His Good Points of Husbandry, ed D. Hartley, 1931, reprinted Bath, 1969

Udal, J. S., *Dorsetshire Folklore*, 1922, reprinted Guernsey, 1970

Wheeler, Homer J., *Manures and Fertilizers*, New York, 1913

Whitney, Annie Weston and Bullock, Caroline Canfield, *Folk-Lore of Maryland*, New York, 1925

Periodicals

Amateur Gardening (London)

Bio-Dynamics: Journal of the Bio-Dynamic Farming & Gardening Association Inc (Stroudsburg, Pa)

Folklore: Journal of the Folklore Society (London)

Garden News (Peterborough, Northamptonshire)

The Henry Doubleday Research Association Newsletter (Braintree, Essex)

Journal of American Folklore (Austin, Texas)

Notes and Queries (London)

Organic Gardening and Farming (Emmaus, Pa)

Popular Gardening (London)

Practical Gardening (London)

Star and Furrow: Journal of the Bio-Dynamic Agricultural Association (Clent, Worcestershire)

ACKNOWLEDGEMENTS

It is a pleasure to record my thanks to the hundreds of generous correspondents in Britain, North America and the Irish Republic who sent me instances of garden beliefs and to the many editors of newspapers and periodicals who published my appeals for information.

I am also indebted to Miss M. H. Spackman for the loan of Kolisko's *The Moon and the Growth of Plants*; to Mrs Muriel Freeman-Taylor for a valuable newspaper cutting; to Mr C. L. Anstine for Baer's planting guide; and to Mr James Stevens-Cox for permission to quote from Doris Cooke's 'An Elizabethan Guernseyman's Manuscript Book of Gardening and Medical Secrets'. My thanks also go to Mr G. F. A. Jackson-Stops and Mr Michael Trinick, The National Trust; Dr David Speller; Viscount Scarsdale; Mr Cecil Atkins and Mr William Brown for notes on Buckinghamshire and Devon beliefs respectively; Mr T. W. Greenslade; Mrs M. C. Baker; Mr John Soper, The Bio-Dynamic Agricultural Association; Ms Bernice Fuller, Traverse City Chamber of Trade, Michigan; The Editor, *Bucks Herald*; and to the Royal Greenwich Observatory.

I should also like to thank Duncan Gray for his help with proofs and Mary Farnell for her skilful preparation of illustrations.

INDEX

Page numbers in italic type refer to illustrations

almanacs, 14

bees and butterflies, 155
birds, 78, 153
bones, 47, 121-5
Burpee, W. Atlee Co, 12, 94, 95, 141

calendar, 70-96, 164
Christmas, 53, 70
companion plants, 157-63
Cross, sign of, 123
curses, 97-103
cuttings, 64-9

Dominion Seed House, 95, 141, 155
Doubleday, Henry, Research Association, 10, 143, 146, 148, 150, 160

Easter, 79-88
evil eye, 66, 97, 121

fall fairs, 93
fences, 23
fertility magic, 43-69
fires, 60
flowers: bees', butterflies', 155; changing colours, 43-6, 80; moon's influence, 20; shows, 93; unseasonable blooming, 132; *see also* plants
fruit-trees: blessing, 91; changing character, 43; cursed, 97, 100; 'griggling', 126, *68*; magic, 43-64;

moon's influence, 20, 24; 'nailing', 55; orchard denizens, 103; planting, 20, 43; respected, 51; told of deaths, 132; unseasonable blooming, 133; wassailing, 53, *49*; weather's influence, 71; whipping, 56; *see also* grafting; harvesting; pruning; trees

ghosts, 104
Good Friday, 80-8
gooseberry shows, 90, *102*
grafting, 20, 43, 54
green fingers, 127, 139

Hallowe'en, 95
harvesting, 22, 23, 27, 46, 72, 150
herbs, 23, 27, 81-4, 158
horseshoes, 48

iron, 115

lawn, 23, 26

manures and fertilizers, 23, 141-55
May, 60, 88
mice, 51, 151
moles, 151
moon's influence, 12-24; fences, 23; flowers, 20; grafting, 20; harvesting, 22; lawns, 23; pruning, 21; trees, 21-4; vegetables, 14-20; weather, 24; weeds, 23, 89, 100

pest deterrents, 142–55; *see also* companion plants; mice; moles

planting and sowing: by stars, 28, 78; by zodiac, 33–42; charms, 43–69; Christmas, 71; compass alignment, 28; day and time, 25, 27; devil's offering, 125; Easter, 79–88; green fingers, 127; influence of sex, 61–4; May, 88; missing row, 65; moon's influence, 12–24; parsley, 81–4; potatoes, 84; rhymes, 64, 125; sacrifices, 46, 126; seedbeds, 63; signs, 77; spring, 73–9; sun's influence, 25–30, 70; trees, 20, 48, 128; weather, 63

plants: bees', butterflies', 153; companion, 157; electricity, 30; empathy, 127–32; 'lightning', 111; music, 135, *101*; pest deterrents, 142–55; prayers, 137; sacrifices, 45–8; sensitivity, 127–41; talking to, 133; told of deaths, 132; unseasonable blooming, 132

plants—individual: alliums, 150, 158; bean, 19, 74, 77, 79, 88, 90, 92, *119*; box, 114, *120*; Calvary clover, 81; cabbage, 17, 64, 161; carrots, 18; chives, 159; Christmas rose, 115; chrysanthemum, 64, *102*; crown imperial, 81; *Cruciferae*, 124; cucumber, 62, 89, 92; cyclamen, 135; *Euphorbia Lathyrus*, 151; garlic, 150; gilliflower, 45, 81; gooseberry, 47, 54, 90, *102*; herbs, 158; horseradish, 23, 162; hydrangea, 45, 116; lettuce, 17; lily, 44, 114, 147, 158; lupin, 154; marigold, 159; nasturtium, 160; nettle, 149; *Nicandra physaloids*, 155; onions, 20, 70, 75, 154, 158; parsley, 81–4; parsnip, 65; pea, 19, 74, *119*; peony, 114; pepper, 65; potato, 18, 22, 29, 46, 76, 78, 84–8, 148, 162; primrose, 44; pumpkin,

75, 95, 134, 161; rhododendron, 45; rhubarb, 150; rose, 75, 79; rosemary 114; sage, 82, *120*; shallot, 71; snapdragon, 114; southernwood, 158; strawberry, 46; tomato, 18, 162; tree-mallow, 114; tulip, 45; turnip, 62, 64, 93; violet, 27; white hellebore, 149; *see also* trees

pruning, 21, 54, 75, 79, *101*

sacrifices, 46, 121

Saints: Bride, 73; Chad, 75; David, 75; Franklin, 89; Gregory, 75; Ice, 76; James, 93; Patrick, 75, 79; Swithin, 92; Thomas, 70; Valentine, 73

salt, 117

seasons, 70–6

seedgrowers, 12, 94, 95, 141, 155

seeds, *see* planting and sowing

sex, influence on plants, 61–4

solstices, 60, 70, 89, 92

stars, 28, 78

Steiner, Rudolf, 10, 16, 36, 149, 160

stones, 100, 118–22

summerhouses, 121

sun's influence, 25, 60, 70, 89, 92

trees: compass alignment, 29; life-index, 130; magical, 106–15; moon's influence, 20, 24; planting, 20, 48–51, 128; planting signs, 77; protective, 106–15; sacrifices to, 47; talking to, 133; *see also* pruning; grafting; trees—individual; fruit-trees

trees—individual: apple, 22, 53–9, 63, 89, 92, 123, 133; ash, 48, 113; dogwood, 76, 109; elder, 109, 148; elm, 116; hawthorn (redhaw), 106; hazel, 123; holly, 111, 129; ivy, 114; Judas tree, 109; lilac, 114; *Mimosa catechu*, 111; mulberry, 77, 113, *120*;

trees—*contd.*
oak, 56; peach, 56, 159; plum, *119*; quince, 113, *120*; redhaw (hawthorn), 106; rowan, 112, *119*; sweetbriar, 114; walnut, 48, 56; willow, 129; *see also,* fruit-trees; plants; trees

vegetables, 14–20, 22, 46, 61–5; *see also,* plants

weather: affects fruit-trees, 71; Christmas and first quarter, 70; crop ripening, 32; influence of tools, 113; May, 89; moon's influence, 24; sowing, 63; spring, 73–9; winter, 95

weeds, 23, 89, 100

White Goddess, 9, 28, 86, 88, 106, 141, 148

witchcraft, 60, 97–126

zodiac, signs, 33–42